The Hunters of Prehistory

The Hunters of Prehistory

by André Leroi-Gourhan
translated by Claire Jacobson

ILLUSTRATED WITH PHOTOGRAPHS AND DIAGRAMS

Atheneum   1989   New York

Atheneum
Macmillan Publishing Company
866 Third Avenue, New York, NY 10022
Collier Macmillan Canada, Inc.
First United States Edition 1989
Printed in the United States of America
Designed by Barbara A. Fitzsimmons
10 9 8 7 6 5 4 3 2 1

Library of Congress Cataloging-in-Publication Data
Leroi-Gourhan, André.
    The hunters of prehistory.
    Translation of: Les chasseurs de la préhistoire.
    Includes index.
    Summary: An archeologist describes how prehistoric
man lived by examining the remains of ancient human
settlements.
    1. Man, Prehistoric. 2. Paleolithic period.
[1. Man, Prehistoric. 2. Archeology] I. Title.
GN740.L4713 1989   936   88–8121
ISBN 0–689–31293–8

Table
of Contents

List
of Illustrations

x / LIST OF ILLUSTRATIONS

Dating of Geological Periods

Primary Era
570 to 225 million years ago

Secondary Era
225 to 70 million years ago

Tertiary Era
70 million to 2 million years ago

Quaternary Era
2 million years ago to present

Translator's Preface

As a participant in the early stages of excavation at Arcy-sur-Cure, I felt a moral obligation, as well as a distinct pleasure, in translating this book. In its original French version it brought back memories of camp life in the early 1950s, when we began digging in the Hyena Cave, which had been discovered in the preceding century. The other cave—Reindeer Cave—was then discernible only from scattered flints and bones found on the surface of a hill. Soil and debris several meters deep had to be removed before the cave, whose roof had caved in in recent times, was found.

I well remember the "baptismal" ceremonial that we, its future excavators, participated in to celebrate what we thought would be discovered as the Reindeer Cave. One of us embodied a reindeer with antlers made from tree branches attached to his forehead. A ritual dance was performed by him, and we drank champagne as part of the ceremony and poured a goodly part of the precious liquid on the ground to honor the occasion.

If some personal note may be introduced, I was half-an-hour away from the discovery of the female Neanderthal jaw, later named "Augustine," which occurred at precisely

6:30 P.M. on a sultry summer day of the year 1952, when I was relieved by Gérard Bailloud, who then proceeded to make the momentous find.

As an American girl presumed to be naive, I was twice enticed into believing I had made a significant discovery in the Hyena Cave, only to have Professor Leroi-Gourhan bend the bone—a rubber bone chewed by dogs—that had been planted in the soil of the cave, in the corner where I was working.

Speleology was a part of our night explorations—we waded through dry and wet, in unchartered parts of caves (a good dozen in Arcy). The engravings in the clay covering wall and ceiling of the Cave of the Horse could only be seen after a twenty-minute crawl from the entrance to the sanctuary. One wonders when we slept . . . for we were up at 7:00 A.M., cheered by a cup of tea and smoked herring and bread.

To quench the curiosity of the inhabitants of the nearby village of Arcy, lectures *(laïus)* were given. I was often chosen to present the latest findings of our excavations, the intricacies of stratigraphy, inferences about the mode of life of Neanderthal man from his remains. . . .

I often spent the early hours of the morning, before my colleagues awoke, reading field notes and looking at the maps and charts located in the work tent, which was erected on the grounds outside the caves—that is where the cleaning and labeling of tools and bones took place. Thus did I memorize what I needed to know to fulfill my *laïus* assignments. The chore of cooking was distributed among all. Three times daily a fire was lit, cooking done, wine poured; shopping in the nearby town was carried out; water from the Cure River was boiled and mixed with wine, the alcohol meant to "purify" the water from contaminants coming from a leather factory upstream. I wonder what good this did, for regularly, every digging season, I came down with the symptoms of a stomach ailment.

We slept in tents—individual or collective—we washed in the Cure, and often swam in it before lunch. We were awakened every morning by the boss's pipes of Pan, gently played at the entrance of each tent. I recall an Easter expedition when we had to sleep in a dry cave up the hill (Trilobite Cave). A fire was lit at the entrance to keep us warm. I slept with my day clothes on, taking off only the outer coveralls and boots, to get into my sleeping bag. A small glass of cognac was a help in falling asleep in the cold. Some of us slept well inside the cave, oblivious of bats and other night life. Thus many days were spent when we literally could not change clothing due to cold and rain.

Our experience can be summarized no better than our leader did thirty years later. In July 1984, on a trip to France, when I visited him at the site at Pincevent, he confided that student excavators nowadays are more serious: They don't have the fun we did at midcentury, though we certainly considered our archeological endeavors serious business.

I wish to dedicate this translation to the memory of André Leroi-Gourhan (d. 1986)—scholar, teacher, friend—who made it possible, and was a leader with an exceptional sense of humor and wit; who lectured us after lunch, with considerable originality, on archeology, technology, geology, history, aesthetics . . . to our educational advantage. I also dedicate the translation to my former co-workers, some of whom became lifelong friends, especially Marie-Claude Chamla, Guy de Beauchène, Jean and Nicole Chavaillon,

Louis Molet; and to Gérard Bailloud and Pierre and Thérèse Poulain; stalwart archeologists all.

Madame Arlette Leroi-Gourhan is remembered for managing the daily routines and for her organizational skills; she was later to become a renowned palynologist. Nanou and Martine, the young daughters of the director, will not be forgotten, for they provided diversion for the excavators and were diligent learners.

I wish to thank Drs. Jacques Bordaz and Louise A. Bordaz for helping with the rendering of technical terms and for their expert examination of the text and editorial retouches.

Finally, Marcia Marshall, my editor at Atheneum, is to be commended for seeing the translation from inception to termination with determination and courage, as many obstacles were strewn in her path.

While I acknowledge the assistance of Jacques and Louise A. Bordaz and Marcia Marshall, the responsibility for the translation rests, of course, with me.

This book was written and later translated in order to arouse an interest in prehistoric archeology in young people across the seas. May it equally stimulate that interest in their elders, in search of a general introduction to the subject. Thus will the labor of love that this translation represents have found its full fruition.

This Preface would not be complete without a tribute to deserving parents. I dedicate this book to my mother and in memory of my father, who shared my joys long distance during my student days in Paris and Arcy-sur-Cure, and who gave me their unfailing love and support in my anthropological endeavors.

Claire Jacobson

The Hunters
of Prehistory

The Hunters of Prehistory

Introduction

We now know that our species appeared on this earth long before there was a written or oral record of it. History is only a thin fringe of a few thousand years at the edge of a period many times longer. During that earlier time Europe was already inhabited by men, our long-ago ancestors.

Who were they? What do we know about them? Imagination, without the help of science, is poorer than we think. Some of the writers and artists who tried to reconstruct the primitive periods of humanity in the last century liked to show creatures resembling Greek statues, living a harmonious existence in the midst of peaceful landscapes.

Other authors pictured our prehistoric ancestor as a kind of gorilla, violent and cruel, almost completely devoid of intelligence and tradition. . . .

Prehistoric archeologists, who work with facts and scientific methods, more and more are able to substitute some degree of certain knowledge and probable hypotheses for these earlier fantasies. Like all specialists, they end up seeing things in a somewhat peculiar manner. Having spent many years studying the earth's record, it is obvious to them that Mauer man, whose only remains are a lower jaw found in

Thousands of years later prehistoric scenes again find favor with artists, but the engraver of 1870 knew little about his ancestors! This cave with a thin and fissured ceiling would not be livable, and a bear would have enough common sense not to attack five men at the same time. This bear, in any case, goes about it very badly; he seems rather to be blessing those present with his left paw. His adversaries are no less strange: The big blond man seems ready to knock out his poor companion, instead of aiming at the bear. Their clothing is elegant but false; the men of the "age of the great bear" wore comfortable sewn clothing and not hide, which is more appropriate for Hercules or Tarzan than for true prehistoric hunters. Finally, the weapons are stranger still. One can argue the hero has picked up a club in his eagerness to rescue a comrade in danger; a good spear would have been better suited. But the axes of the other two are toys: A bit of flint badly attached to a stick surely would not have been useful in a real hunt, and prehistoric men, wisely, were more dependent on their spears with ivory points. We can only approve of the figure in the shadow who watched this senseless scene with prudent reserve.

Science has progressed in the hundred years since this engraving was made, and we understand more clearly how prehistoric men lived. . . . (Photograph Musée de l'Homme, from Louis Figuier, "L'Homme primitif," Paris 1870)

Heidelberg, lived two hundred thousand to five hundred thousand years ago, while the cave paintings of Lascaux only date back to fifteen thousand years ago; almost, it could be said, the day before yesterday.

In our cave site at Arcy-sur-Cure near Paris we found our "Augustine," and we can picture her seated on the stone where she just sat down before the last ice age. Augustine was a poor housekeeper, and we find remains of mammoth in all the corners where her broom neglected to sweep. Augustine is known to us only by half a jaw, but what a jaw! She could have broken the leg of a reindeer in one bite. This is enough to give her a strong personality.

If you should ever wish to scrape the soil in a cave, I hope you will remember that you don't discover an "Augustine" by housebreaking. You don't penetrate the secrets of prehistoric people by wielding a pickax. They reveal themselves only by clues, and, as in a detective story, you can no longer follow the sense of the clues if, for example, you've emptied the ashtray that contained the revealing cigarette stub.

If everything were as simple as these pages may sometimes give the impression, there would no longer be a mystery, there would be no need for prehistorians. On the other hand, you should not be fooled by the apparent complexity of a modern excavation: numerous maps, hundreds of pages of notes, chemical analyses, small pieces of bone, and flint samples of all kinds. If it wasn't possible to find a way through all this material, the science of prehistory could not have begun or have progressed.

What interests us above all is to try to understand what Augustine, her husband, and their contemporaries did with their ten fingers during the long winter evenings, in the

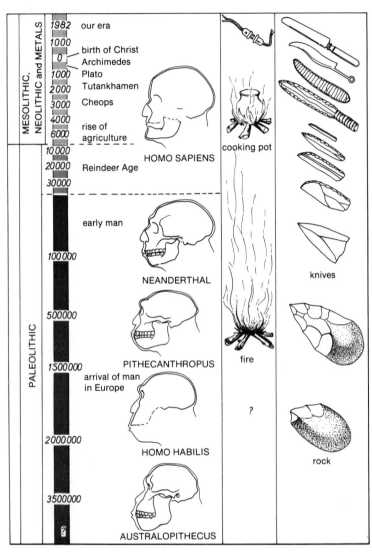

MESOLITHIC, NEOLITHIC and METALS	1982	our era	
	1000		
	0	birth of Christ	
		Archimedes	
	1000	Plato	
		Tutankhamen	
	2000		
	3000	Cheops	
	4000		
		rise of	
	6000	agriculture	
			cooking pot
	10 000	HOMO SAPIENS	
	20000	Reindeer Age	
	30000		
		early man	
	100 000		
		NEANDERTHAL	knives
PALEOLITHIC	500000		
	1500000	PITHECANTHROPUS	fire
		arrival of man in Europe	
	2000000		?
		HOMO HABILIS	rock
	3500000		
	?	AUSTRALOPITHECUS	

In this chart, we can see the vast difference between historic times (approximately 5,000 years) and prehistoric times (more than 2 million years). We see how much time it took to progress from fire to cooking pot, and we see the continuity of a tool like the knife, which, through time, became more and more advanced.

depths of the cave. Certainly, they worked hard to earn the minimum number of woolly rhinoceros and wild horse necessary for life, and they worked better than one might think. We unjustly tend to reject these Neanderthal men with the low skull and heavy jaws, just like a lord of high birth who ignores the fact that the grandfather of the first baron plowed the land. We would prefer to trace our family tree

When we discovered the first fragment of Mousterian man, one of our group had the idea of baptizing her "Augustine," so that we did not constantly have to repeat: "The portion of mandible from a very ancient paleoanthropian, of level 20 in the square A9 of the Hyena Cave at Arcy-sur-Cure," which is rather tiring. Here, we see a maxillary and the mandible, and, to the left, comparable bones from a modern man. A jaw is a small thing, but over the years we were excavating in this cave, we had already learned a great deal about its prehistoric inhabitants; only this skeletal trace of the ancient tenant had been lacking, and a picturesque first name to bring our heroine back to life again. (Photograph A. Leroi-Gourhan)

 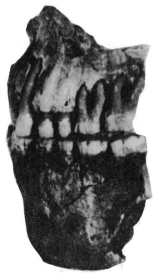

back to the painters who decorated the walls of famous caves, forgetting that these artists would have not been able to create if their earlier cousins with the low foreheads had not amassed knowledge for many previous millennia, which they passed on to following generations.

We have no problem admitting that twentieth-century science was derived from the science of the nineteenth, and so forth, all the way back to the Greeks. But what about before then?

Before, it was the *Bronze Age* and, before the Bronze Age, it was the *Neolithic,* the period of the first farmers, and we can still picture these farmers as the distant ancestors of Greek philosophers. But before that?

Before that, there was the *Reindeer Age.* Only reindeer hunters and salmon fishermen existed. They had the same face as ours and they knew how to sculpt bisons in stone. Yet they seem quite far removed from us, and it is only with effort that we can see that their way of life had an influence on modern society. But before that, what then?

Before, there were hunters; but those early hunters did not exactly resemble humans of today. The most ancient of these are often described as kinds of higher monkeys. It seems almost impossible to believe that the scientists of the Atomic Age owe anything to this monkeylike *Pithecan-thropus.* Yet this is so. If there had been even the smallest gap in the slow acquisition of essential technology in this distant past, we would have had to start all over again. We don't always think enough about the continuity of the link that joins us to an inaccessible past. We vaguely imagine that the prehistoric man struck stones at random to make miserable tools and then, one day, contemporary man entered the stage of history and everything changed.

Nothing is more false. Our classical world is only a few thousand years old, but to prepare for it, man had developed over at least two million years. The marvels of modern science are the fruit of a long growing period, and we shall see in these pages that the breakers of flint with the low foreheads and the heavy jaws knew, as well as we do, how to choose their raw material, design a program for manufacture, and produce mass artifacts.

1
How Prehistory
Is Interpreted

There are few sciences that are as easy to approach as prehistory and whose data are more current and accessible. Prehistoric men left behind in the soil millions of stones they had worked. In many places, it's been easy to dig into the earth to discover the bones and ashes that are the remains of ancient human settlements.

And yet, we no more study prehistory by collecting chipped handaxes than we study botany by collecting lettuce. The earth is a marvelous book; unfortunately, time has dog-eared and ravaged it, and it is written in a difficult language, much more difficult to learn than the languages of old parchments. But reading parchments tells only a small part of our history. To know the rest, we have no other choice but to bend over the subsoil and to attempt to read it.

A little more than a century has elapsed since prehistorians first attempted this deciphering. Today we know a considerable amount of the faraway past of humanity. But to get this far took a great deal of patience and ingenuity.

Documentation

The surface of the earth is affected by two contrary forces, well-known to geologists. On the one hand, rocks are corroded by wind, ice, and water: This is what is known as *erosion.* On the other hand, the products of erosion, carried along by water's downward trickling, are deposited in certain places in successive layers: That is *sedimentation.*

For the two or three million years that are of interest to us in this book, we have to be concerned only with the most recent past of earth's geology, which includes the birth of mountains and the formation of marine sedimentary layers, reaching several kilometers in depth. The history of the earth itself amounts to billions of years. When the first man

Here we have created a beautiful prehistoric site, typical of those that really exist. A cave rests under the modern landscape, but the ceiling has partly collapsed and is covered by slope deposits. The "book of the earth" is here, protected by thick meters of debris.

appeared on this planet, the continents and seas were already approximately the same as they are today.

But since the time that man appeared, erosion has continued to scour the mountains. The rubble on the heights has slowly made its way down to the valleys; stone boulders have been transformed into pebbles, then into gravel, sand, and, finally, silt. The means of transportation is water: rain that, from channel to brooklet, from brooklet to brook, to stream, to large river, draws the soil toward the sea, millimeter by millimeter.

If we could place a camera in front of a landscape and take a picture every one hundred years, the film would show how the moving parts of the soil slide down the slopes and disappear into streams.

The film would also show that this displacement doesn't work in an even and continuous manner. There are times of rest for the moving materials, when they settle in fissures, on level spots, and in the depths of valleys. Then one day they will be taken up and washed down farther. Prehistoric sites are found in places where sedimentary layers have stayed in place without too much damage.

Let us imagine, for example, the well-sheltered corner of a cliff beneath an overhang, a little above a river. Some men have selected this as a shelter in which to live. They eat animals, throw away the gnawed bones, leave behind broken flint knives, light up fires to heat themselves. One day they leave. The cliff continues to crumble gently through the action of the frost. In a few years, the hunters' modest remains will be covered by a layer of stones and mud. Centuries or millennia later, other hunters will take notice of the same rock shelter and stop in turn, unaware of their predecessors whose traces are buried under their feet. They will depart again, leaving behind other debris, characteristic of their way of life, which stones and mud will again cover. And so on, until the day when a last flow of rubble will definitely level the shelter, closing the cover on this book of the past.

Other men, during this time, settled on the beaches of rivers. Generation after generation of flooding covered their broken weapons, lost objects, and garbage heaps with layers of mud and sand.

Everywhere our ancestors lived, layers of sediments have imprisoned a bit of their history, from the oldest chapters to the most recent. But quite often, too, erosion has intervened. It has displaced sediments, it has taken away everything or mixed it up. The archives of the earth do not resemble a modern book, but rather an old manuscript that is torn and faded. Nowhere do we find the complete story of the human adventure, from the first to the last line: only here and there a part of a page, sometimes a few chapters that are linked together, but which have to be matched with other bits of the work.

Prehistoric sites

A prehistoric site, among the millions of places where man has lived, is a place that has more or less escaped the ravages of time. These sites are few in proportion to the surface of the earth. And all of them do not contain the same kinds of documents.

What are some of these documents? In order to understand more clearly, look at the house where you live and imagine it being abandoned, just as it is, for several thousand years. The most perishable materials will disappear very rapidly: The roast on the table will be only bones; curtains will rot and crumble in turn; only a small pile of nails and metal parts will remain from the table; from the bed only a bundle of springs. In the end the house will cave in on the whole lot. There will remain only stones, broken glass, chipped dishes, rust, shapeless odds and ends, to excite the curiosity of future archeologists. These items will pose many problems if the scientists wish to reconstruct a picture of a family evening gathering in this house, when it was still alive. What was the use of this rod with these copper rings? Was it a toy, a game? And these strange springs: Were they women's bracelets, the main part of a machine to throw projectiles, or decorations for a hat?

If you can truly imagine what the things you have abandoned would become, you are ready to understand prehistory—a fascinating science, but one that requires caution—you are capable of imagining what can be found in a prehistoric site and how it can be interpreted.

In layers recently laid down—that is to say, by going back to approximately the year 2000 B.C.—bone and metal (iron or bronze) objects are found, as well as pottery, stone objects, sometimes wood objects, very rarely textiles, consumed animal bones in abundance, less often human graves.

The layers that go back to 8000 years B.C. contain the same remains, but instead of metal, which was not yet known, chipped or polished stones are found.

Going back farther, that is during the whole Reindeer Age, the list is reduced to bone objects, chipped stones, animal bones, and, sometimes, the bones of human beings.

At many sites, only objects of stone and a small number of bone bits are to be found. Bones this old survive only as

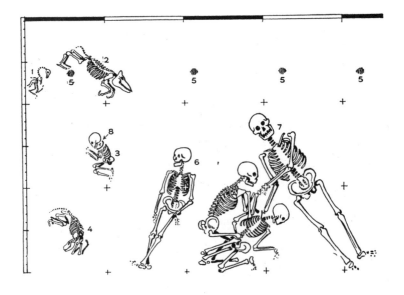

an exception. If bones lasted forever, we would live in the midst of millions of dinosaur skeletons, as well as skeletons of mammoths and whales. Under normal conditions, bone is rapidly decomposed and retrieved by nature.

So, we shall try to reconstruct the life of prehistoric man on the basis of the scanty evidence mentioned above.

There are different kinds of sites. The most frequently encountered are the ones in the sand and mud deposited by streams, or in the wind- or waterborne silt deposits that cover slopes. Many chipped stone tools found in these sediments have lost all links with their original environment, but during the last few years discoveries have been made in France of a few habitats in the open air, which escaped natural destruction. Unfortunately, most of these remnants of the periods of prehistory have been destroyed by mining, deep plowing, and large irrigation works.

Caves and *rock shelters* contain sites that are just as precious. A cave is like a box, holding and protecting a prehistoric site. This protection is not absolute; it does not

Let's imagine that this peaceful family of Montagnards from Vietnam is hit by a sudden cataclysm. What would remain of them for the prehistorian? (Photograph Gabille). The bottom picture shows us the result of such event as the prehistorian would excavate and record it. We see the skeletons of a chicken, a pig, a dog; the skeletons of a child, a woman, a man, and two adolescents; traces left by posts set in the earth; but the only indication of the life they led, the only object that survived, is the silver necklace of the child. If the bones had been absorbed by the soil, as most often happens, this scene of peasants, rather comfortably equipped, would be reduced to only a necklace.

always prevent disturbances; but it's often effective and sometimes miraculous. Unfortunately, caves are grouped in only a few regions and many of them have already been ransacked by collectors or amateur archeologists. For science, the protection of caves is as important as the protection of manuscripts in archives. But while it would not occur to anybody to read an old manuscript without knowing Latin, many people imagine that it is enough just to open the earth to know what is underneath.

Peat bogs and *lakes* conserve even wood objects, leaves, and seeds. Thanks to the objects found in bogs, we know about the life of the first peasants, 4,000 years ago.

Recent layers in the earth or a little below are not really relevant to prehistory. But they may contain burials, hut floors, or ovens for pottery firing or to melt metal from the last periods before written history.

Prehistoric settlements on the surface are innumerable. When erosion is gentle, it sweeps soil along toward streams, leaving chipped stones behind on the surface. We find them in fields, at plowing time. But these sites have generally not kept anything besides chipped stones, and often objects of different periods are all mixed up. Thus, for science, they are a secondary resource, like a manuscript whose letters were cut out and scattered at random.

Deciphering the manuscript: excavation

Let's continue with our comparison. To read an old manuscript, we must turn the pages slowly, one by one, settle down before each page, and, taking all the time necessary, seek to understand the very difficult text we have before our eyes.

The principle of excavation is the same. We must uncover each level as completely as possible, *without changing the place of anything.* When we have spread out this great "page" of earth with all that is on it, we have to take notes, photographs, drawings, trying to understand everything we see. Each grain of earth, each bit of charcoal, each formless stone fragment is as important as the most beautiful chipped flint points. To scrape the earth and take out only the objects that please us would be the same as to copy a text while taking only nouns and abandoning articles, pronouns, and verbs.

It is only when we have finished deciphering the first layer that we can gather the objects found, lay aside samples and evidence necessary for research, and go down to the next level. All this work demands a great deal of time, patience, and also the appropriate materials. A pickaxe isn't necessarily the proper tool to read the earth. To understand, grain by grain, the earth upon which his ancestors walked, the prehistorian is most often armed only with scrapers, tweezers, and brushes.

What's most important is to prevent the escape of the smallest clue. The plans and photographs must be complete enough to record the details of the position of each trace, the least fragment worthy of interest. Then all the useful samples must be taken and classified; for here our comparison with a manuscript ceases to be entirely valid. With a manuscript, one can go back and ponder again a passage already read. On the other hand, the earth is a book whose pages are destroyed as we turn them; we can read it only once in its original text; when the earth of the layer is taken out, all that has not been carefully transcribed is lost forever.

Each sample taken will be the object of particular study.

An excavation in a Mousterian layer. The remains are carefully dug out with very small tools and left in place for later examination. Here we see remains of cave hyenas, wild horse, and mammoth. (Photograph J. Vertut)

The objects made by man, such as chipped stones, will be given to a specialist in *typology,* who will compare them with previous finds. Human bones will go to the *physical anthropologist,* who will define the type of man to whom they belonged. The *paleontologist* will take care of animal bones; he will help, especially, to define the climate of the period in which they lived. He will also determine the different species found at the site, while attempting to distinguish those species eaten by man from those that came to die here naturally. The *palynologist* will look for the fossilized pollens of plants of the period in small samples of earth. Larger soil samples will be handed over to the *geologist,* who will trace the history of sedimentation and erosion in the place where they were gathered. He will find particles brought by water and wind, as well as traces of great cold periods, and many other details that will permit a better understanding of the climate and the conditions of life, while the *geomorphologist*

All prehistoric people did not live in caves. Here is the tent site of Magdalenian reindeer hunters in northern France. The soil is strewn with hundreds of flints, bones, and hearthstones split by fire. The group of stones and charcoal, on the left, is the hearth. To the right, the different black spots indicate places where ashes were emptied from the hearth and mixed with domestic refuse. (Photograph A. Leroi-Gourhan)

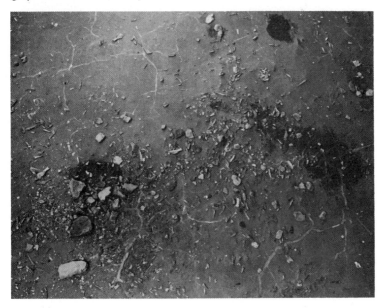

*The "book of the earth" seen in cross section. The drawing repre-
sents a schematic cross section of a cave site, where we see layers
of successive cave-ins of the roof, hearths (marked by crosses), big
bones at level 5, and at level 10 the tusks of a mammoth.*

will reconstruct the landscape of the period. The fragments of carbonized wood will be studied by the *botanist* and *physicist;* the former will identify plants that were used for heating; the latter, by radiocarbon dating, will give an idea of the age of the layer.

Using all means possible, we will attempt not to lose one comma of the prehistoric text. We will expose it to ultraviolet rays, infrared rays, to detect what our eyes have missed in ordinary light. When, finally, a layer is destroyed to expose the one underneath, we will have done everything to save the text of this first page of the record.

Yet we'll excavate only part of the site, so that, twenty years or several centuries from now, the prehistorians of the future, who may have more advanced scientific means, may take up the puzzle again.

How the evidence is used
Now we have information on the stone tools, animals, plants, climate, and people of several superimposed soil layers. We have no written clues, and few notions of the place in time of the various bits of information: the number of years, centuries or millennia that separate them from one another. We don't know the names of these peoples, their chieftains, their gods. Nothing remains of their language, their ideas, their music. The small bits that have come down to us bring only meager information about their material life. It's as if we were asked to draw the uniform of a soldier—our only clue the button from one of his pockets.

Simplifying a little, let's see how prehistorians have managed to decipher a faraway past with what looks like discouraging means.

Scientists began to think seriously about what those chipped flints found in the ground could mean in the middle of the nineteenth century. At this time, the facts seemed to illustrate the following theory of prehistory: The flints could only be tools that belonged to men; and, since they were buried at a certain depth, it was because they were very old. On the other hand, these stones were accompanied by bones of mammoth, reindeer, and several animal species, either extinct or no longer living in our climate. They reached the conclusion that man, long ago, lived in a different climate from that of today and made stone-chipped weapons and tools.

These first findings opened new horizons on the origins of humanity. They were enough to fire the minds of men during the whole of the last third of the nineteenth century.

But a second version of these facts, ours, is more complex. Let us suppose that we have to study several batches of chipped stones spread out over time. Each batch differs from the preceding one. There are several "styles," which seem to have succeeded one another. Each style was given a name that recalls, in general, the geographic location of a prehistoric site in France. We thus have, for example, in France, three groups that belong to the following styles:

1. Acheulian, from Saint-Acheul north of Paris

2. Solutrean, from Solutré in eastern France

3. Chassean, from Chassey-le-Camp, also in the east

We also have groups of animals whose bones were found in the corresponding periods. For our examples they are:

1. Early elephant, Merck rhinoceros, giant fallow deer

2. Mammoth, wooly rhinoceros, reindeer

3. Red deer, beaver, domesticated pig

These animals represent more or less the following climates:

1. A temperate climate with extinct animals
2. A cold climate with some extinct animals
3. A temperate climate with some domesticated animals

The study of fossil pollens reveals the following plants for the three groups:

1. Wild grape vine, box shrub
2. Birch, willow
3. Oak, beech

Soil samples also give us information:

1. An old beach of a stream
2. A slope of clayey silt and fragments of limestone that has been split apart under the effect of frost
3. A rocky spur in a forest environment

Finally, we have information on men of that same or neighboring periods: skeletons, sculptures, engravings on bone or rock.

This is only a general example. But it already shows how we read the text of our prehistoric archives: by coordinating the documents of each period, by comparing the periods, and by confronting all these bits of truth with corresponding facts about other parts of the world during that time.

2

Climate
and Environment

Near the beginning of the last century, the great French naturalist Cuvier studied bones that had been found in the ground and proved that they belonged to animals of extinct species. Even better, beginning with the few fragments he possessed, he succeeded in reconstructing these strange beasts. And he demonstrated that they had surely lived in the midst of a vegetation and under conditions very different from those we know today in these same regions.

Thus, when prehistorians constructed their new science, they were already familiar with the idea that nature and climate had been subject to profound changes in the distant past. They knew of the great extinct species and which lived during the same time period, and they knew how to classify them in chronological order. What was most striking was that the animals that lived in France in those very ancient times had the characteristics of animals living in a nearly tropical climate.

When other French scientists showed that men lived in France from the beginning of the Pleistocene Epoch, 600,000 years ago, they were confronted by the opponents of prehistory. These opponents were not upset that animals had existed in our regions, since the fact was accepted, but rather about the ancient origins of the human species, which until that time were supposed to have appeared far more recently.

After the discovery of elephant remains accompanied by chipped flints in the river deposits, cave excavations revealed at least as strange an animal mix, made up of reindeer, bisons, polar foxes, musk oxen. France had known not only a nearly tropical climate, but also one close to that of Lapland. And the idea rapidly grew that not only had man been the contemporary of extinct large animals, but also that he had lived through considerable changes in climate.

How did these changes come about? The advances in geology, at the beginning of the twentieth century, showed that climatic evolution had been very complex. From the beginning of life on earth, climate underwent important periodical change, characterized especially by successive heating and cooling. For the Pleistocene Epoch, and for the last part of the Pliocene, prehistorians first believed that the climatic variations had been enormous. But they soon understood that in temperate regions and with a mountainous topography, such as France has, a difference of less than ten degrees in average annual temperature was enough to completely change the range of glaciers and the location of animal and plant species.

When the average temperature rises or falls, the pattern of rains also changes. When it rains more, erosion is more rapid; when it rains less, erosion slows down. This way climatic differences are registered, almost automatically, in the layers of sediment. This is why we first of all study the earth that covers prehistoric sites.

Strata and glacial periods

In order to understand how the earth's layers were formed, we'll show the history of a great river, because it's here that erosion plays an important part.

Water comes down from mountains and marks out a track to the sea. If large movements of the earth's crust do not change the height of mountains and plains, our river deepens its valley, to lower its level to reach that of the sea.

Let's suppose that the average temperature drops. Glaciers immediately spread: The Alps, Pyrenees, all the north of Europe is covered by a heavy cap of ice, such as the one that covers Greenland today. The amount of water captured in the ice is enough to lower the sea level by several dozen meters. The lowered river speeds its rate of deepening and clears a valley with sharp slopes. But now, after thousands of years, the average temperature rises again. The glaciers melt and retreat, the sea level rises. The river runs less rapidly and abandons along the way part of the silt that, when it flowed faster, it had dragged into the sea. The silt fills the lower part of its valley, forming large alluvial plains. When a long cold period returns, the sea level is again lowered, the river deepens and runs more rapidly, and the alluvial plain remains like a terrace suspended above the river. Climatic variations happen again a number of times. The river continues to lower its level, leaving stepped terraces along its banks. Each terrace corresponds to a period of warmer climate, to an *interglacial* period. The older terraces are at the top, the most recent on the water's edge.

In its turn, the glacier, which is a river of ice, registers its advances and retreats by leaving behind moraine deposits: long banks of rock and gravel sediment.

Finally, the sea beach, too, records evidence of its movements in the form of ancient beaches, some perched above the current coastline, others buried under the water.

Geologists have studied all these layers of strata of very different materials, large, medium, or small, swirled by the water or layered by the slow progression of glaciers, burst by ice, polished by the wind. They have tried to understand the subtle orchestration of climate changes registered in them. Reading strata is quite difficult because things do not happen as simply as in our theoretical scheme. Other phenomena have intervened, numerous local events have confused the picture. Here the earth rose slowly, then erosion took away a whole episode; elsewhere, a part of the river changed course and the strata correspond to this change, not to a climatic one. Finally, as this whole evolution happened before historic times, we have no clue to tell us whether the cross sections of one region correspond to the same time periods as the cross sections of another.

The result is that scientists still do not agree on the number of glacial periods and the time of the smaller changes of secondary climate. Still, it has been customary to assume that there have been four great periods during which glaciers covered a large part of the surface of continents. These four successive glaciations have been given the names of four small tributaries of the Danube River in southeastern Europe, where their traces were studied for the first time: *Günz, Mindel, Riss,* and *Würm.* Observations made on the terraces above rivers have been compared with those made on ocean beaches, to establish which layers might have come from the same fluctuations of climate. For the Günz and Mindel Glaciations, which are the oldest, comparisons are difficult. For the Riss they are more certain. For the Würm relationships are relatively well established. The time of the Riss Glaciation, the Riss-Würm Interglaciation, and the Würm Glaciation, perhaps altogether 200,000 years, corresponds to the period of the development of the direct ancestors of our culture: Neanderthal man and contemporary *Homo sapiens.*

Plants

Marvelously, microscopic grains of pollen resist the forces of destruction. In a peaty soil, the best of conditions, they last without change for tens of thousands of years. Each year, millions and millions of these little grains, carried on winds, spread over the soil. A botanist can easily identify the plants from which these grains come by examining them under a microscope. The pollen indicates, with near certainty, the climate in the period when it was deposited on a layer of the earth. This is because the life of each species of wild plant is narrowly limited to the climate suitable to it; plants do not have an animal's alternative of fleeing the winter cold or migrating according to the seasons. It is enough to know how the plant species succeeded one another in a given region to reconstruct exactly the climatic variations there.

In order to establish pollen diagrams of strata, it's necessary to take cross-section samples of the earth, one centimeter apart if necessary, being careful that current pollens do not mix with the samples. Under the microscope it's possible to establish the exact proportion, in each sample, of pine trees in relation to birch or hazel, for example, or the relation of fern to dandelion. From layer to layer, we are able to see when one of these species disappears or, on the other hand, makes gains over the others.

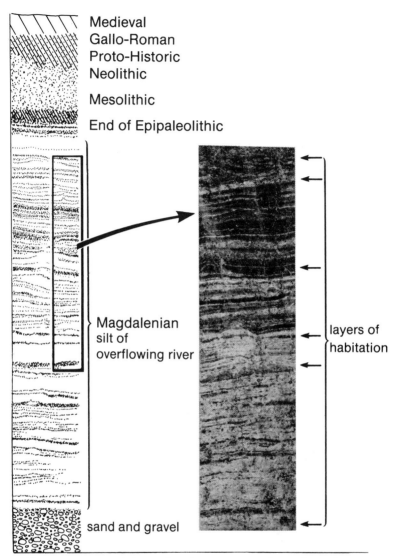

Medieval
Gallo-Roman
Proto-Historic
Neolithic

Mesolithic

End of Epipaleolithic

Magdalenian
silt of
overflowing river

layers of
habitation

sand and gravel

This cross section of the earth at Pincevent was chosen for its long, uninterrupted time span and because the levels of the periods discussed in this book are well represented. The thin layers of alternating silt and sand create a time line that shows the relative ages of the documents that were found.

The different plant compositions that we discover in each layer of the soil do not only reflect climate changes. They also reveal something of the landscape of the time: here the humid forest, there steppes, elsewhere sparse woods (called by scientists "parkland").

Thus, thanks to geology and botany, which are complementary, we already have the means, in the sites favorable to this type of research, to reconstruct very precisely the life conditions of ancient animals and man.

Research on the plants of the Pleistocene Epoch has shown, first of all, that except for several rather cold peaks, climate variations were not so extreme as we'd first supposed when it was discovered that the same region had been inhabited by reindeer and elephants in succession. For example, the average temperature of Orléans in central France during glacial periods was more or less that of Copenhagen, Denmark, today; and, in the hottest part of the interglacial periods, the temperature was no warmer than today in Seville, Spain. In addition, it is necessary to remember that though the average temperature of a region has varied, its latitude has always remained the same. The sun always climbs higher in the sky of Orléans than in that of Copenhagen to the north. In many regions, the differences in climate linked to variations in temperature and humidity may have been less pronounced than comparisons with today's geography would lead us to believe. On the other hand, there was a great deal of cooling off in the regions where glaciers descended into deep valleys where the sun seldom shone.

It is the distinctive topography of France that played the greatest role in glacial periods; we see that, even in sunny summers, a lowering of temperature could create the enormous ice masses that advanced up to the shores of the Rhône River.

During the great cold period of the Würm Glaciation, which we know a little better than other glaciations, France must have offered a very complex botanical picture. Alpine plants grew down to the low plains, and vast expanses of cold steppe covered entire regions, while the plants of the interglacial period, similar to today's plants, continued to grow in regions farther away from glaciers. We shall see that it was the same for animal species; in certain periods, the chamois was the neighbor of the reindeer and wild horse.

Animals
For periods before the Würm Glaciation, the distribution of animal species is known to us only generally. But beginning with the Würm Glaciation it's possible to see the distribution in a relatively precise manner. We know the kinds of game prehistoric man hunted and which species among these animals were most abundant. We even have illustrated evidence of some of their hunts, such as the famous wild oxen in the Lascaux cave paintings of southwestern France.

When we examine soil layers at the beginning of the Pleistocene Epoch we don't find an exact relationship between the succession of climatic periods and that of animal species. It seems that the warm-climate animals of the beginning of the Pleistocene were succeeded by "colder and colder" animals, the coldest appearing at the end of the Würm Glaciation, to be then replaced by today's fauna. At the end of the Pliocene there was, in Europe, an extraordinary variety of animals. Troops of mastodons, wild horses, elephants, zebras, hippopotamuses lived on the plains and in the rivers of France. Large fallow deer, bear, rhinoceros, saber-toothed tigers, and giant beavers rested in the shadow of oaks and walnut trees. The period geologists classify as the beginning of the Pleistocene brings only slight change in this variety: The saber-toothed tigers and mastodons disappear, while elephants and other species continue to thrive.

On first sight, it seems surprising that, although the climate was not very different from today's, France was home to an African-type fauna, with hippopotamuses and rhinoceroses. But, in reality, these animals are no more African than European. It is only that they survived in Africa, while they

During most of the Pleistocene Epoch, the primary game was not reindeer, but wild horse and aurochs. In the Lascaux Cave, prehistoric man painted the most extraordinary figures of aurochs, which are the direct ancestors of some of our domestic cattle. (Photograph A. Leroi-Gourhan)

disappeared from Europe. There are two explanations for this. First of all, in Africa, climate might have changed from tropical to equatorial, a difference not fatal to large animals. In Europe, the difference between a mild, temperate climate and the cold of glacial periods was no greater, but the cold was enough to kill many animals.

The second reason was that in Europe man—that is, the hunter—was present more or less everywhere, while in Africa he left great spaces uninhabited, at least by him. A good xample of the ravages of man on animal species is that lions, rhinoceroses, and tapirs lived until recently in Asia, in climates similar to ours. They disappeared, exterminated not by natural conditions, but by man. And in Central Asia, in Siberia, where winters are far harsher than in France, tigers and panthers still remain.

The bones of small mammals, such as rodents, and the shells of mollusks mark climatic variations more closely and show animal evolution in a more precise way than the great mammals.

We find the periods that left us the most documents on prehistoric man are after the Riss Glaciation. By this time, giant beavers, saber-toothed tigers, and hippopotamuses had been gone from the scene for a long time. What game did our faraway ancestors hunt? To get an idea, let us imagine western Europe during the intermediate period between the Riss and Würm Glaciations, at a time when the climate was similar to today's, with the same plants growing in the same regions.

All the way in the north, toward Scandinavia and northern Russia, the *tundra* rules, a cold grassland covered with lichens, and the *taiga,* a swampy forest with elm trees, birches, and pine trees. The tundra and taiga are populated by mammoths, reindeer, and wild oxen. Wolf packs and wolverines live off these animals when they do not attack smaller prey: lemmings (a kind of field vole), arctic hare, and ptarmigan—which are also the normal prey of the blue fox and snowy owl. Except for the mammoth, all these animals still exist today in Siberia or Canada.

To the south of this region, the big *forests* of evergreens and trees with leaves begin. The main inhabitants of the evergreen forests are elk, marten, squirrel; the leafy forest shelters deer, bison, and a few woolly rhinoceroses. Woolly rhinoceroses and mammoths seem to have traveled between the tundra and the forest.

If we go farther south, the landscape becomes differentiated. In western Europe, it is still the leafy forest crossed by fields, known as "parkland"; in central Europe the great *steppes* begin, which reach northern China. Immense herds of wild oxen, known as aurochs, and horses roam the steppes and the park in the north, with mammoth, woolly rhinoceros, sometimes reindeer. The saiga antelope and some marmot live in the cold steppes.

France, during the interglacial period, was divided, like today, into forests, fields, and mountains, with a vegetation similar to that of today. In the forests, red deer, fallow deer, roe deer, and boar lived; in the fields lived horses and aurochs, the *Elephas antiquus*, and Merck rhinoceros, an animal closer to today's rhinoceros than to the woolly. In the south there were wild donkeys. The mountains were inhabited by the ibex and chamois and marmot. Perhaps, all the way south, the last hippopotamus survived.

All these herbivores were hunted by numerous carnivores:

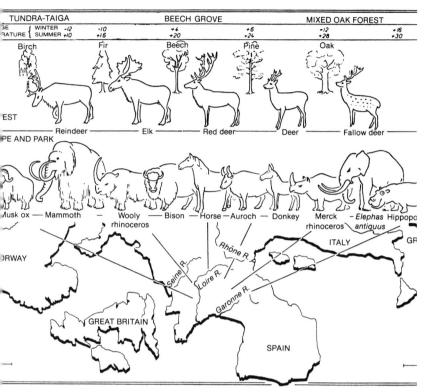

Pictured here are the different groups of animals characteristic of the different climates in southwest France.

smaller wolves than in the north, wild dogs, lions, panthers, and, in the forests, lynx. Brown bears, similar to those of today, were numerous, as were the cave bears, today extinct. The cave bears were very variable in size. Some were hardly bigger than a Great Dane, while the giants of the species, standing on their hind legs, might stand four feet high. These cave bears, which were probably not very carnivorous, lived in groups in the limestone hills and retired into caves to hibernate.

We see that the animals of the period between the Riss and Würm Glaciations lived in climates comparable to today's:

The northern fauna with, notably, reindeer, mammoth, musk-ox.

The fauna of the forest and northern steppes with elk, mammoth, woolly rhinoceros, bison.

The fauna of forests and temperate steppes, with horses, aurochs, red deer, and roe deer.

Along the Mediterranean, the same animals, plus *Elephas antiquus*, Merck rhinoceros, fallow deer, and donkeys.

More than a hundred thousand years have passed since then, yet the majority of species still exist. Only the mammoth, *Elephas antiquus*, woolly rhinoceros, Merck rhinoceros, and the cave bear have disappeared. Man is probably responsible for their extinction: These large animals presented an easy target for human hunters, who were more numerous and better armed.

The wild horse was the preferred game in all periods of prehistory. Several races of horses existed, which were adapted to different climates, so that during temperate periods as well as during the cooler ones, we discover the horse at practically all sites. This drawing is from the Lascaux Cave in the Dordogne.

The reindeer didn't live in France during all periods of prehistory, but each cooling of the climate brought its immense herds back to the region.

The list of small mammals—field mice, field voles, squirrels, foxes, badgers—has not changed much nor that of the innumerable birds—from the eagle to the vulture and wren. The giant penguin was exterminated only a century ago.

This does not mean that all these animals were exactly the same as their contemporary descendants. In a thousand centuries, lions, horses, reindeer have evolved, but so little that, if we could see an auroch from before the Würm Glaciation and a contemporary Spanish bull side by side, we might seriously hesitate before telling them apart.

We have seen that climatic variations during the course of the Pleistocene were less dramatic than we had first thought when discovering traces of the glacial periods. Even so, these variations determined changes in the distribution of plant species, and these changes led to animal migrations. When specific plants moved to the north or south, they drew along the animals that ate them. If we could have remained seated on the shores of the Loire River from the end of the Riss Glaciation until the end of the Würm Glaciation, we would have seen pass by, at thousands of years intervals, toward the north, first reindeer and mammoths, then elks, then horses and aurochs, and, finally, giant fallow deer and *Elephas antiquus.* After the cold returned rapidly at the start of the Würm Glaciation, we would have seen these animals taking the road south, with reindeer settling for long centuries on the shores of the Loire. Hardly a thousand years before modern times, when the Würm Glaciation ended, we could have seen the great migration start again toward the north. But this time, when red deer, aurochs, and horses reappeared on the Loire, they were no longer accompanied by elephants and rhinoceroses. Horses and aurochs returned very near the time when man would take them away from the great grasslands to lead them to the cattle shed and stable.

The reconstruction of the environmental past

By patiently assembling thousands of precise details drawn from the excavation of pebbles, river sands, cave clay, traces of fossil plants or pollens, from the smallest tooth of a small animal, by counting one by one the thin layers of clay abandoned by the glaciers each season, by drawing maps, by cross-checking all the findings obtained, prehistory, the science that we first thought was impossible, has already given us a true picture of the past of the human species.

But what do we know?

During the last half-century, the length of time man and his ancestors were known to have existed in geological history grew ever longer. Thanks to the efforts of physicists (radiocarbon dating), of paleontologists and geologists (stratigraphy), we see the appearance of the first anthropians, human ancestors, a million, perhaps even three million years ago. We cannot be more precise, but two or three hundred thousand years more or less change nothing in our sense of the marvelous range of the human adventure.

We also know that our distant ancestors, in France, sometimes lived among elephant and reindeer. But these elephants did not know banana trees; they grazed on oak trees. And these reindeer never knew the long polar night. The contrasts in climate were not extraordinary. It was enough that the average temperature during the whole year was lowered by ten or twelve degrees for the elephants to be replaced by mammoths, for the oak forests to withdraw to Italy and Spain, for the Mont Blanc Glaciers in the Alps to block the Saône River near Lyons in southern France.

The exact succession of climates and animal species remains obscure at the beginning of the Pleistocene Epoch. But starting with the Riss Glaciation, we can picture things more and more clearly. Except for a few large mammals, all existing animals are still found today between the polar circle and the latitude of Algeria. During the intermediate period between the Riss and Würm Glaciations, the species that lived in France were those one finds today in the southern half of this zone. During the Würm Glaciation, the species were the ones found today in the northern half. Naturally, the boundaries are never as precise in reality. There were mixtures of the two kinds of fauna in some regions, and we must take into account differences of latitude: The last elephants could live near the Mediterranean, at the same time as waves of mammoths and reindeer invaded northern France. Our prehistoric setting is now well delineated. We need only to have the principal actor, man, enter the scene.

3

The Human Record

The skeletal remains of prehistoric animals are not abundant: Only half a molar may exist from a herd of elephants. Men were fewer than elephants and their skeletons are more fragile. The whole of the human remains found in a century of research in all of Europe takes truly little room. With careful packing, all the bones from before the Riss Glaciation can be contained in a weekend suitcase. For the intermediate period between the Riss and Würm Glaciations a footlocker would be ample. For the first part of the Würm Glaciation we would need a trunk; for the second part, three or four crates. Even so, the remains we have found are not complete. When a stroke of luck gives us a jaw, the whole skull is lacking; if by chance we find a cranial cap, the face is missing. For the period before the Riss Glaciation, there do not exist enough pieces of skull to reconstruct a single complete one. Until the Würm Glaciation, there is not one skeleton to accompany the three or four more or less intact skulls that we possess. For the Würm Glaciation we are a little richer: We have real skeletons that are practically complete.

These materials, although small in number, are still eloquent. By studying them thoroughly, we know, at least in general, the appearance of the first men.

The first discoveries showed us our ancestors as beings with low foreheads and projecting mouths, very apelike in appearance. Heated quarrels revolved around these remains. Some saw in man a monkey who had brilliantly succeeded in crossing zoological rungs; others thought that those poor creatures with the low forehead were not quite man and that our ancestors remained to be discovered. The discussion became an attack on, or defense of, religion; the voices of those who really knew the documents were joined by others, less competent, who did not add self-control and clarity to the consideration of the problem of the origin of man.

When the first remains of Neanderthal man were discovered in a Rhine valley, with its low skull and its projecting eye sockets, we imagined that we had found the perfect intermediary between the gorilla and contemporary man. But as discoveries followed one another, this intermediary position was given to another ancestor, *Pithecanthropus,* and more recently to *Australopithecus.* We have since found beings much more primitive than Neanderthal man, and yet closer to us in time! And we shall see that poor Neanderthal was worth more than his flat skull would lead us to think.

The study of our ancestors begins with the fossilized remains of their skeletons. These remains are often only a single tooth, fragments of a skull or other bones. During the last dozens of years the discoveries of numerous fossils in south and southeast Africa have upset earlier ideas on the origin of man. Instead of this monkey with the large brain that would have progressively acquired an upright posture, we found instead man with a small brain but who was upright, like contemporary man: Australopithecus, whose oldest remains go back three million years.

These Australopithecines already split pebbles to obtain flakes with a cutting edge. They had hands that were not used for walking. They were neither quadrupedal like the horse, nor four-handed like monkeys; rather they walked upright and manufactured tools. A trail of footsteps has even been discovered, on a soil that, at the time, was soft. And two and a half million years ago, this early man existed alongside another anthropian whose skull was discovered later. This fossil was much more human than Australopithecus; it is known as *Homo habilis*. Its brain is far more developed than that of the Australopithecines and its tool kit more advanced.

A general outline of human evolution

We know that during the Primary Period, 570 to 225 million years ago, some vertebrates freed themselves from their original sea environment. They acquired lungs to enable them to breathe in the air. They reached solid earth and they became quadrupeds. We don't know the intermediary forms of this transition. But today there still exist many fish that can use the oxygen in air and spend long hours away from water, dragging themselves from marsh to marsh during the dry season.

These first inhabitants of solid earth became differentiated into two branches: the amphibians, or batrachians, and the reptiles. The Secondary Period, 225 to 70 million years ago, had enormous reptiles, such as *Brontosaurus* and *Diplodocus*. Yet we have to remember that these famous giants never reached the size of the large whales of today. Side by side with these monsters, there lived, during the second half of the Secondary Period, other smaller reptiles, the size of rats or dogs. Their legs were longer, some had hair and were probably warm-blooded. Their teeth had become diversified (incisors, canines, and molars). In short, their biological characteristics and general appearance brought them close to primitive mammals, and it is likely that toward the end of the Secondary Period, the first so-called mammals evolved from this group of reptiles, the mammals that were to dominate nature during the whole of the Tertiary Period 70 million to 2 million years ago.

These primitive mammals, at first very small and poorly defined in their characteristics, became diversified from the beginning of the Tertiary Period and even that early tended to divide into modern groups of herbivores, carnivores, and such. Certain lines already appear to lead directly to horses and other ruminants. Other lines end in felines or hyenas. We can imagine the existence of such ancestors when, starting with modern-day types, we go backward in time. Thus, the ancestor of the horse seems to us to be the animal that, in a certain earlier period, comes closest to it by its adaptation to running and by its horse-like diet. Adaptation can be explained in different ways, but it is an incontrovertible fact. A mammal from the beginning of the Tertiary, whose diet and way of life (herbivorous, a grazing animal that did not chew its cud like a cow, living in the large spaces of the steppe) resembled those of future horses, would normally become, in its descendants, today's concept of the horse. A really striking fact is that many of the necessary conditions in reaching "horsedom" appeared at least twice in two different animal lineages: horses themselves, and a strange mammal from South America, the thoatherium, which, starting from an entirely different stock, became extinct after developing almost all horse characteristics.

This last example is important. It helps us understand one of the difficulties in the problem of man's origin. Among the fossils of creatures leading toward humanity, we can not distinguish with certainty those who really reached humanity and thus are our true ancestors, and those who might have evolved along parallel lines without reaching the human state.

Among the primitive mammals that would develop into today's species, we find the early representatives of *primates.* At the beginning of the Tertiary Period there is very little difference among them. They have a generalized tooth pattern for their varied diet of fruit, shoots, and insects; they have five fingers on each limb, small stature, a generalized skeleton, not specially adapted either to running or to life exclusively in trees.

But the other line of mammals will progress by specializing in different directions. Teeth will become rasps for grass, millstones for grain, files and knives for meat. Limbs will become adapted to rapid running and jumping; toes will become smaller, fuse with one another, to end up as the feet of horses, oxen, pigs.

Only primates will remain strangely stationary, not evolving in each of these essential traits. This apparent stagnation is one of the most striking traits of their nature. They will retain, until man, the possibility of eating everything, of moving their limbs in all directions, of using their twenty fingers, of sitting erect or rising on hind legs. The evolution of primates will occur in one particular direction: the expansion of the volume of the brain. Thanks to this brain, primates will better use a body not perfectly adapted to any particular action, but one that is able to carry out all of them.

Not all primates followed this route with equal success. Today we find evidence for other routes, from the lemurs with small brains to the chimpanzees. But toward the middle of the Tertiary Period, there appear the first representatives of a vast group that will be the source of superior kinds of primates: that is, the anthropoids, Australopithecines, and anthropians.

The anthropoids probably stem from several origins whose branches end today with the gorilla, chimpanzee, orangutan, and gibbon. They all show a fairly strong development of the brain, but (at least for the forms known up to now) they keep a semiquadrupedal (four-footed) posture and many characteristics of true monkeys.

In 1924, the first *Australopithecus* was discovered in South Africa. Discoveries were made all over Africa, and today we possess several skulls and parts of skeletons, even a sample pelvis, a bone that is clearly different in an anthropoid and in man.

Not only was *Australopithecus*'s brain proportionally more developed than the brains of anthropoids, but its teeth are that of man, with small canines and—unique among primates—*Australopithecus* walks upright, like man. *Australopithecus* is classified with man. Characterized as "austral monkey" (*pithecus* is the Greco-Latin word for monkey) at the beginning of its career, the names given later on to discoveries of different samples reveal the growing attention given to them by paleontologists: *Paranthropus* (akin to man), *Zinjanthropus* (man of Zinj), *Homo habilis* (dextrous man). We do not know how far back Australopithecines go.

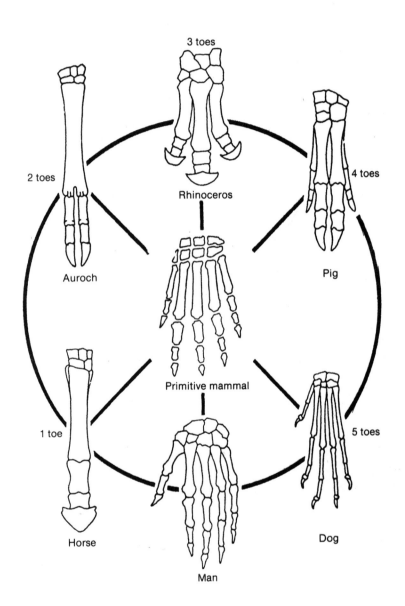

3 toes

Rhinoceros

2 toes

Auroch

4 toes

Pig

Primitive mammal

1 toe

Horse

Man

5 toes

Dog

OPPOSITE

In the center is the hand of a mammal of the beginning of the Tertiary Period (70 million to 2 million years ago). Around it are the front paws of contemporary mammals more and more specialized for locomotion. In order, from the dog, which still has five fingers but a useless thumb, to the pig, with four fingers, to the rhinoceros, with three fingers, to the ox, with two fingers, to, finally, the horse, which has only one working finger. At the bottom, a human hand seems strangely near that of the primitive mammal. This hand, which certain reptiles of the Primary Period already possessed, has improved and increased in the flexibility of all its joints to make itself the faithful servant of the brain of man.

Here are the skulls of two of the great ancestors of man. To the left, the reconstruction of the Australopithecus *at Sterkfontein; to the right, the skull of* Homo habilis *at Koobi Fora, who represents one of the oldest individuals of the human species. Despite many more primitive characteristics, this fossil is a very near ancestor of the archanthropians.*

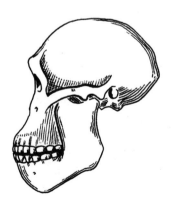 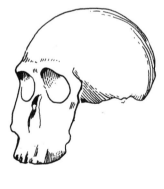

Certainly at least to the second half of the Pliocene (which lasted two to twelve million years).

Are they our direct ancestors?

The question is unnecessary, for however the process of the development of the species took place, the result is the same: man.

Australopithecines' form puts them in the position of ancestors of man because they show, at a still-primitive stage, the three characteristics that only they share with man: front teeth that are comparatively weak, a face that is rather flat, and the ability to walk in an upright position. Australopithecines themselves also had ancestors, who are as poorly known to us as Australopithecines themselves were a generation ago.

People or gorillas?: anthropians

Anthropians is the name we have given to all primate fossils that not only walked upright and had a developed brain, but who also left indisputable traces of their ability to manufacture tools. All of them appear to have had enough mental development to pass the process of toolmaking from one individual to another. The production of tools assumes, as we shall see below, the ability to preserve technological knowledge, which has nothing in common with the habits of animals.

We divide the anthropians into three groups: the archanthropians, paleoanthropians, and neanthropians. How these groups succeeded over time is not clear; their periods of presence on the earth have even overlapped.

Very ancient members of the human family: the archanthropians *(Homo erectus)*
The remains of archanthropians are few and they were found in widely separated regions. By order of discovery, *Pithecanthropus* in Java; *Sinanthropus* near Peking; *Atlanthropus* in Algeria; the Mauer jaw in Germany; the occipital bone of Verteszöllös in Hungary; the skull of Tautavel in France. Considerable distance separates these different fossils in time, as well as space, which shows how widely spread the archanthropian stage became. The name "Prehominids" has often been applied to these creatures, but we prefer "archanthropians," which means "very old members of the family of men." It is very difficult to say just where humanity begins, and we just don't know enough about these creatures to decide whether they were "prehuman" or "human." They knew the use of fire and manufactured tools. Their brain was approximately twice as large as the brain of a gorilla, but it did not reach the volume of ours. Their teeth and their face showed a stage of development in between.

Sinanthropus *("Peking man")* is a very close relative of the pithecanthropines. It was discovered in China and completes the map of the Old World's archanthropians.

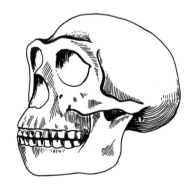

The last primitives: paleoanthropians

If the archanthropians are rare and dispersed, the paleoan-thropians are quite numerous, although caves usually ideal for preserving fossils were emptied of their precious remains before the Würm Glaciation because of variations of water level during the glacial and interglacial periods.

The remains of paleoanthropians found prior to the Riss Glacier are few and very different from each other. Among them we might place the Mauer jaw, although many scientists believe it is really archanthropian. Its position in the soil layers shows that it lived in a mild enough period for the hippopotamus, for bones of this animal were found in the same layer.

The incomplete skull caps of Swanscombe (England) and Fontéchevade (France) are more recent, but it's difficult, on

The famous Mauer jaw, found near Heidelberg, Germany. Unfortunately, only the jaw remains, and it closely resembles an archanthropian or a pre-Neanderthal jaw, especially the one of the famous skull of Tautavel. It is a contemporary of the oldest chipped flints of Europe, and its teeth are quite similar to those of Neanderthal man, so that, despite its unprepossessing features, scientists agree that it is indeed the jaw of a man.

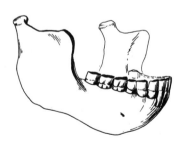

the basis of such incomplete remains, to infer very much. The Steinheim skull (Germany), that of Saccopastore (Italy), that of Gibraltar, have the same general appearance: rounded skull, enormous brow ridges, large round eye sockets, a brain about the size of modern man's. Several of these skulls discovered in the Near East show more characteristics of *Homo sapiens.*

Paleoanthropians visited caves, and some of these have preserved their contents so well that we can find remains that include skulls, long bones, and a few more or less complete skeletons. The paleoanthropians can be divided into several subgroups, with variations most often in the structure of the face and the shape of the skull. Their brain was about the same size as ours, but the frontal bone still carried the heavy brow ridge shared by all anthropians except *Homo sapiens.* The reduction of this ridge goes hand in hand with the development of the brain and a bulge in the forehead's frontal bone. Among paleoanthropians, the most important and best-known group is that of Neanderthal man. We do not have to ask whether paleoanthropians are men or still super gorillas. They are clearly men, and their works testify to a human sense of technical creation.

Neanderthals

It was one hundred and twenty-five years ago that the famous Neanderthal skull cap was discovered, and it played a historic role in those debates on the origin of man in the nineteenth and first quarter of the twentieth centuries. Neanderthal man's body was not much different than that of contemporary man; it seems only to have had a rather massive torso and rather short and muscular limbs. It did not show the characteristics even the scientific literature gave it: curved back, thick neck, long hanging arms, separated big toe. . . . On the other hand, its skull showed deep differences with the other paleoanthropians. The brow ridges are present; they are united with a frontal bone that has a rather small bulge, but one that is quite visible. A very surprising fact is that those whose brain capacity could be measured have brains surpassing in volume the average for contemporary man (1,600 cm³ compared to 1,500 cm³ for contemporary man). This large brain, where the proportion of different parts could be studied, thanks to the molds of the cranial cavity, is very little different from ours, except for the back of the skull, which is more developed, and the frontal area, less developed. In addition, the flat skull accentuates the "primitive" look. Neanderthal man's face was without cheekbones and his cheeks continued without a break from the eye to the junction of the lips, but his jaws didn't protrude much. His teeth were of the same general shape as ours but much bigger; the canines are of normal size in proportion to the other teeth.

Neanderthal bones were found in various sites in Europe and Asia: in Teshik Tash, central Asia, and in Shanidar (Iraq), where a large cave was discovered with several Neanderthals buried in it. One of them had been laid down over a bed of flowers, a moving testimonial of the feelings of his companions. This detail was disclosed by soil samples collected around the skeleton; this soil contained great numbers of spring flower pollens.

In Croatia (Yugoslavia) the site at Krapina revealed the broken and partially buried remains of fifteen individuals, who were the contents of one or several cannibal banquets.

In France, Neanderthal remains are numerous. The major part of these fossils consists of fragments (such as the Augustine lower jaw of Arcy-sur-Cure), but there are skulls accompanied by more or less complete skeletal parts in the southwest region. Neanderthal remains have also been found in Belgium (Spy) and Italy (Mount Circeo). The customs of Neanderthal man are a little better known to us than those of his predecessors. Those who lived in caves do not appear to have had a well-developed sense of comfort. Yet in the caves of Arcy-sur-Cure, France, where the author of this book worked, the layers above the level where Augustine lived show a clear evolution toward cleanliness; the central part of the cave was fairly well cleared of big debris and trash: It was covered instead with flint tools and bone tool fragments.

The tools of Neanderthals are often very carefully chipped, not at all inferior to those of neanthropians, who followed Neanderthal. They knew the art of butchery: When they carved, their early knives left cuts on reindeer or horse bones at points chosen very carefully. We can distinguish, for example, the places where Neanderthal man cut in order to skin a reindeer from those where he cut the tendons to dismember bones.

In considering the customs of the last Neanderthals who lived in France, it becomes rather difficult to see them as an intermediary form between monkeys and man, as some had formerly thought. The man of La Chapelle-aux-Saints, and that of La Ferrassie were buried by their peers, which probably means they had some sort of religion. Pieces of red ochre, fossil skulls, and curiously shaped stones have also been found in the caves of the late Neanderthal. This tendency to collect curios marks the first beginning of an artistic sense.

The intellectual level of the Neanderthal was certainly superior to what might be surmised by the shape of his skull. His end might be imagined two ways. How did paleoanthropians become extinct? When did the neanthropians appear? When we study the different sites where remains of the Upper Paleolithic directly follow the Middle, a definite break becomes clear between paleoanthropians and the following neanthropians, between the Neanderthal and Cro-Magnon, symbol of *Homo sapiens.*

The skull of La Chapelle-aux-Saints to the left. This is one of the best preserved of the complete skulls of a Neanderthal. To the right, the skull of the famous "old man of Cro-Magnon," from the Dordogne in southwest France. Though he does not have any teeth, he was not that old when he died—probably in his fifties. And in addition, he was covered with a crust of granular calcite and had lost a large piece of his jaw when found. Yet it is he who stands for "Cro-Magnon man," the painter and sculptor of the Reindeer Age, and he is so close to us that only specialists can tell him from modern man.

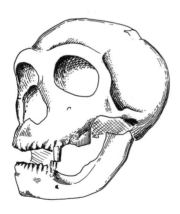 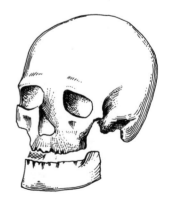

It looks as though *Homo sapiens* had in one fell swoop eliminated his rival. But if we consider the paleoanthropian-neanthropian ensemble as a unique block, lasting one hundred thousand years, the break is much less definite. The characteristics that show the contrast between paleoanthropians and neanthropians essentially affect the skull:

Paleoanthropians	*Neanthropians*
-brow ridge	-no ridge
-large "circular" eye sockets	-long "rectangular" eye sockets
-no canine tooth depression	-canine tooth depressions
-large teeth	-"sapiens" teeth
-low skull	-"sapiens" skull
-flat bone at back of skull	-bulging bone at back of skull

These different characteristics are combined in various ways. As we have only a few complete skulls, we can say that almost all subjects have individual differences, from the ones closest to the paleoanthropian model (Gibraltar, Saccopastore, Steinheim) to those that show only traces of the paleoanthropian type (Syria, Lebanon). Thus the question of whether *Homo sapiens* and Neanderthal man existed together is difficult to answer. The extinction of the paleoanthropians, like that of the mammoth, must have happened through the effects of many different causes. *Homo sapiens* perhaps had a direct and brutal involvement in their extinction, but it may have been along with natural causes.

The discovery of Australopithecines led to knowledge of creatures of almost model primitiveness. In contrast, archanthropians and paleoanthropians were closer to contemporary man. The sequence *"Homo habilis–Homo erectus–Homo sapiens"* led to getting rid of "pithecus" (monkey) from the names and gave a new label to early creatures already developing into man. Attempts were made to improve the image of the Neanderthal: His name was changed to *Homo sapiens neanderthalensis.* This made him, in relative terms, a kind of first cousin, which would certainly have pleased him. But the term *Homo sapiens* calls us immodestly "man of wisdom." We then decided to call ourselves *"Homo sapiens sapiens,"* something like"the man of the wisdom of wisdoms," a fancy title, but very clumsy.

One period remains, one that is poorly pictured, which (about 30,000 years ago) marks the beginning of the Upper Paleolithic. In France it certainly existed in several regions and is illustrated by a culture with the name "Chatelperronian," from the town Chatelperron. It is particularly well represented at Arcy-sur-Cure. There, men lived on the porch of what we called the Reindeer Cave, where they constructed round huts made of stones and mammoth tusks. They worked ivory and bone for their hunting gear and domestic activity (javelin points, awls, picks . . .). From flint they made blades fashioned according to the technique of the Upper Paleolithic, but a part of their flint was still worked "in an older Neanderthal style" from which they

A map of the major discoveries of paleoanthropians in Europe. We see that the remains are unequally distributed. As expected, we find them rarely in northern Germany and England, or in the high mountains, because climate there was probably unfavorable to the settlement of man. In other regions, limestone caves insured the preservation of bones. If we take into account the areas that were favorable or unfavorable to settlement, we see that the paleoanthropians had already settled the larger part of western Europe.

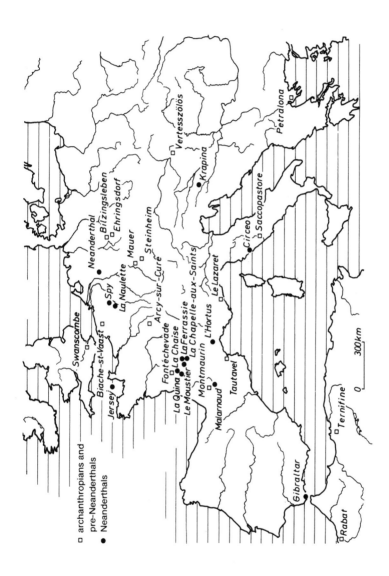

archanthropians and
pre-Neanderthals
Neanderthals

made tools in that ancient tradition (side scrapers). The red dye ochre (ferrous oxide) was used extensively. They manufactured pendants from bone or ivory and put holes in the roots of the teeth of fox, marmot, bear to hang as adornment. Everything about the Chatelperronian leads us to consider it as the first signs of the culture of the Upper Paleolithic, and some scientists think "Upper Paleolithic" equals *"Homo sapiens."* But the human teeth gathered at Arcy-sur-Cure and the skeleton excavated at Saint-Césaire are from Neanderthal man! The transition from "barbarian" to "modern" is made by men who clearly retain Neanderthal characteristics.

Our fellow humans: the neanthropians

Other people appeared one day in France, similar to ourselves. Where did they come from? We don't know, because well-dated skeletons are very rare; but it seems as though the distribution of today's races goes back far in time, and although the evidence is reduced to only a few individuals out of whole populations, races were, except for a few cases, already settled on their respective continents.

4
Culture

We now know that the span of human time is immense, that it covers several geological periods and several changes in climate and fauna. We know that during each period there lived human beings different from ourselves.

We are now going to study all these men, taking as a guide not so much the shape of their skulls, but what remains of their works. Since the creation of tools (technology) is one of the most distinctive characteristics of humanity, we can find no better guide.

What is most striking in this cultural development is that it progressed, from the most simple to the most complex, during all of time, independently of races and groups. We can trace the whole history of human technology without having to study the history of skeletons; whether he was a near-monkey or a genius, the first artisan, starting at zero, could do nothing more than break a rock into two to make a knife. His successor, hundreds of thousand years later, even if he were mentally inferior, profited from everything that was discovered before him. Nonmaterial creations, such as songs, rites, social or religious principles, can become extinct or be born again from one period to another; the tool itself sums up and keeps alive for us the thoughts of all preceding generations. Each generation inherits a solid technological base upon which it can live even without changing it, if it lacks imagination. But the least spark of creative intelligence will enrich it, by adding something new.

To describe completely the cultures that succeeded one another during the course of the Pleistocene Epoch, we need to picture:

-the means of subsistence of man (hunting, fishing, food gathering)

-his means of protection (clothing, housing)

-his social organization

-his religious and artistic concerns

Even for the most ancient peoples who have left written testimony, it is often very difficult to draw this picture without gaps. Let's see how we can get along with our few prehistoric documents.

Some bring direct evidence. Thus, according to the manner in which they manufactured flints, we can surely know the degree of technological development reached by the men who lived in a specific place and period. Other documents bring indirect evidence. For example, when we find—hidden in a cranny in the depths of a cave difficult to enter—an engraving representing a mammoth, we may suppose that the artist who drew it did not choose such a place only to be able to work in peace; he looked for mystery, which is an indication of religious or magical thought.

Objects often do not give any information except the technological. We find a flint point; we reconstruct the process by which it was manufactured. Good. But what was its use? Here the scientist enters into the realm of knowledgeable guesswork. Was this flint a knife? Or more probably the head of a spear? An awl? We shall never know for sure. A prehistorian shall never be able to say, for instance: "This point was used by a woman to cut out leather strips from a musk ox, which formed the upper part of the moccasins of male reindeer skin, which were the footgear of men going to trap partridges in the spring snow. . . ."

For many years scientists have used microscopes to study traces of wear and tear on the cutting edge of flints, and the researchers of several countries appear to be on the point of being able to diagnose, with the microscope, the characteristic wear and tear from cutting hides, meat, reindeer antler, wood, or bones.

All this does not mean that prehistorians are reduced to only their imagination in order to reconstruct the mode of life of our remote ancestors. Luckily, indirect evidence exists that is strong enough for us to be able to interpret it cautiously. Here are a few examples:

If we find a human skeleton lying on a bed of powdered red ochre, as happened several times, it is probable that it is related to some sort of ritual.

If we find pierced shells, we might think adornment certainly played a role, although the type of adornment may not be known: necklace, bracelet, embroidered clothing, or amulet.

If, next to pierced shells, we find stones of strange shape, pieces of mineral, samples of rock crystal, we can think that men collected those objects because they found them beautiful and they attributed magical properties to them. Today, among traditional peoples who make similar collections, these two motives still exist.

Finally, since no people during the Pleistocene were engaged in agriculture, we can assume that there were no cities, not even gatherings of hundreds of individuals, during long periods of time. Humans who exist by hunting and fishing must live in small groups. A maximum of five reindeer can live all year on a square kilometer of tundra. To feed a man, we have to be able to count on about ten reindeer per year. We can also estimate twenty kilometers as the maximum distance slaughtered animals could be transported, and the number of animals hunters killed as one in ten. If we take into account all these data and also such factors as bad years and epidemics, we conclude that, under the best of circumstances, in the Age of the Reindeer an area of 1,500 square kilometers could not support a group of more than fifty individuals year round. Yet even this group would have had to split into small bands of ten to fifteen in order to best use its hunting grounds.

These calculations are naturally approximate. They are based on the present conditions of the reindeer hunt and do not take into account either fishing, or the hunting of other animals, or the gathering of wild plants. Nevertheless, they indicate that, under the best conditions, human groups could not have been very large. By using direct or indirect evidence, scientists have to be on constant guard to keep imagination under control; its role is to guide research, not to take its place.

We tried to show on this chart the different areas of prehistoric knowledge. For time spans we had to use a logarithmic scale, because we would have needed several meters to give the real proportions of the Quaternary Period. Thus the Acheulian seems equivalent to the Neolithic and Bronze Ages, while it really lasted a hundred times longer.

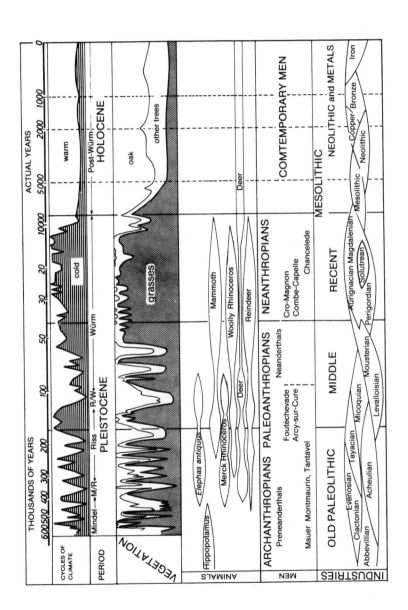

5

The Beginning of Toolmaking

Before primitive men, the earth belonged only to animals. Very intelligent monkeys could have picked up a branch to loosen fruit, but they never manufactured tools. The first creative labor was the work of the most ancient of men.

We can imagine these men, in France, living in a slightly warmer climate than ours. Although most of the wild plants were the same as today, landscapes were very different. There does not exist in the temperate zone a square meter of soil whose appearance was not altered by man in the years since those ancient times. Today only some deserted parts of Argentina or the northern slopes of Tibet can give us an idea of the immense fertile spaces of an unconstrained nature in the temperate zone.

According to the seasons, an important part of the food supply was insured by chestnuts, hazelnuts, acorns, beech nuts, numerous shoots, roots, tubers, and tender bark. Later on, most of these foods lost their importance in the diet of our regions, as new plants were imported.

The hippopotamus, the elephant, the rhinoceros were perhaps too big to serve as animals of prey for the first hunters. But they discovered various kinds of deer. Horses and boars were abundant. Rivers and swamps offered them fish and turtles. It wouldn't be too fanciful to picture this area, for its first inhabitants, as a sort of earthly paradise; predators were numerous, and there were winters much like those today in Italy and the Riviera. But the quest for food must have been relatively easy.

One of the human fossils we can attribute to this first period was discovered near Heidelberg, Germany—the Mauer jaw, already mentioned. A jaw amounts to little with which to reconstruct a man; nevertheless it is enough to give an idea of size, facial proportions, tongue muscles, the lower part of its face, and even, up to a point, its diet.

The Mauer hominid was of a normal human size, neither gigantic nor minuscule. It was a paleoanthropian or an evolved archanthropian; that is, a creature more evolved than *Pithecanthropus,* for example, less evolved, however, than Neanderthal man. The jawbone is enormous, without a chin, with the traces of very powerful chewing muscles, but with little trace of the small muscles that move the face. Quite big by themselves, the teeth appear rather small if we consider them in relation to the enormous jaw that holds them. The canines are not large. As a whole, they are omnivorous human teeth. We know nothing about the brain. All that can be said is that the Mauer creature stood erect, was heavily built, had a heavy face of little expression. If we added more detail to it, we would risk giving free rein to our imagination.

Unfortunately, no tool was found near the Mauer jaw. It was lying in a sand quarry, among numerous remains of elephants, horses, bears, lions, and even saber-toothed tigers. But in other layers elsewhere dating from the same period, we find, in France (notably, in Abbeville) and in England (notably in Clacton-on-Sea), chipped flints. With the Mauer jaw and the flints of Abbeville and Clacton, we shall try to bring this culture alive. There is, however, particularly in Africa, plentiful evidence of even more ancient Pebble Culture (with tools made from rounded stones) at the extreme limit of humanity's history, at least two million years ago. But before we go ahead, it is important to distinguish what we do know from what we only suppose:

1. We have no proof that Mauer man manufactured tools, since none were found near its jaw. But it is probable that he manufactured them, because *Pithecanthropus* and *Sinanthropus*, which had a more primitive jaw than Mauer's, already manufactured pebble tools; in Algeria, the remains of *Atlanthropus* have been found near a beautiful set of tools of the Clacto-Abbevillian type (those found in Abbeville and Clacton-on-Sea).

2. Perhaps the makers of Abbevillian and Clactonian tools were not similar to Mauer man. Here we advance no argument pro or con. But if Mauer man manufactured flints, he was capable at least of making tools much like those of Abbeville and Clacton. Indeed, the manner in which these tools were manufactured is the most primitive one can imagine, when a man breaks a rock to give it a cutting edge.

Thus, our first summary can be set forth: Western Europe, at the beginning of the Pleistocene, was inhabited by men of whom one at least (whose jaw was recovered) was a primitive paleoanthropian. These men manufactured tools according to the elementary technique of Abbevillian and Clactonian flints. We know nothing more about the men. Let us see what the tools themselves disclose.

Primitive techniques

We are on the edge of a river. Floods have eroded the river shores; in the cross section of the soil we see pebbles and blocks of flint. Let's take a large, heavy stone, which will serve as a *hammerstone,* and also choose a good flint pebble, two or three kilograms in weight. We will hit the pebble vertically with the hammer stone, using great force, on the flat surface near its edge. The piece knocked off is a large flake, thick and irregular, but with very sharp edges. We can repeat this several times on the same pebble: Each time we'll break off an irregular, thick flake, with an oblique striking platform and a large *percussion bulb.* This is a Clactonian flake. This flake is the simplest product of human industry.

We can imagine human beings who would be content to hit large pebbles and make enough Clactonian flakes to dismember game or manufacture a wooden club. But in fact,

First step: By perpendicularly striking the flat side of a pebble, we detach a Clactonian flake, which can serve as a knife.

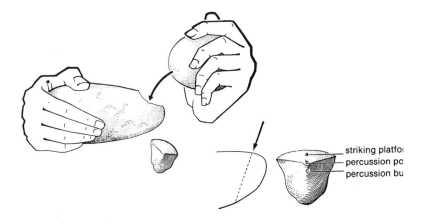

striking platfo
percussion po
percussion bu

when one breaks pebbles in this way, in addition to flakes, there finally remains what's left of the stone, the core or nucleus, which has become a cutting tool as well. Thus, the most primitive industries have generally left two types of tools: Clactonian flakes and core tools.

Core tools

Now let's choose a flat pebble, weighing approximately one kilogram. Let's take off two Clactonian flakes side by side from one of the flat surfaces of the pebble. We get a kind of *chopper.* If we turn the chopper over and hit it on the ridge left by the two flakes, it gives us a *chopping tool,* a kind of knife with a very wavy cutting edge. This clearly is a more complex procedure.

We can continue our work on the other side of the pebble at the smaller end. By knocking off two or three flakes on each edge here, we create a point: The tool has become a *biface,* also called a hand axe. It is a knife with a crude edge, but sharp and long enough for the simple uses that were asked of it. The biface is the characteristic tool of the prehistoric industry of Abbeville.

We have just run through a catalog of the most primitive human creations: Clactonian flake, chopper, elementary biface. These objects are found, together or separately, in almost all well-preserved sites of the beginning of the Quaternary Period. To manufacture them, you need only choose a pebble or a flint nodule of the proper shape and chip it by means of several blows with a hammer applied perpendicularly to the flat surfaces. But as simple as the procedure is, it is very much beyond what a monkey could do. As soon as the worker must turn the stone around to chip the other surfaces, he must make a judgment. In choosing the places

Second step: By detaching two or three Clactonian flakes, the pebble becomes a "chopper."

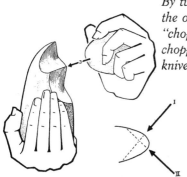

By turning it around and striking the other side, we can make a "chopping tool." The chopper and chopping tool are very primitive knives.

Third step: By making a point on the chopping tool with a few blows, we create a hand axe, still large and heavy, but pointed and with a cutting edge. This is the type of biface that characterizes the Abbevillian.

to hit to create a point, the worker must possess a real sense of the structure of matter and be able to control the force of the blows; in a word, he must have foresight.

Let's imagine that today all technical knowledge were to be suddenly lost and that men had to start again. They would probably need several centuries to rediscover the use of flint; then, for generations, they would be able to make only the objects that can be fashioned without too much apprenticeship, that is, Clactonian flakes; then they would come to choppers, finally to discover the excellent cutting properties of the biface.

We have just seen that a specific group of procedures gives birth to a family of tools. From the flake to the chopper, from the chopper to the primitive biface, there is progress. Progress is possible because the series of procedures was

A. A pebble chipped to produce a cutting edge. This is the oldest manufactured tool (chopper), and it is found in many different periods.
B. The oldest bifaces, still irregular, evolve from the primitive chopper into a pointed tool.

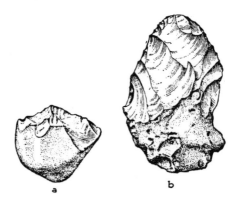

a   b

preserved from generation to generation. It is the first known technological tradition. From the day it was established and maintained, the brain's capacity was no longer so important. If the workers had the minimum humanity necessary to manufacture tools, they were already capable of transmitting a technological tradition without changing it, until the day when some genius of a successor, of the same race or a different race, invented a new procedure and created new forms, which would in turn pass into tradition.

6

The First Artists

The period of the Abbeville and Clacton industry was followed by a harsh glacial period, perhaps that of Mindel. The hippopotamuses definitely disappeared from our regions, and with them other animals too sensitive to cold.

What happened to the men of the preceding period during this time? We hardly know anything about them. Surprising as it may seem, we have found only rare evidence dating from the Mindel Glaciation. Yet, if we compare the remains from before this glaciation with those from afterward, we discover (and this is no less surprising) that they fit together perfectly, as if there had been no break, neither in the industry nor in human types. Tools exactly follow the Abbevillian and Clactonian tradition; and among fossils we find archanthropians similar to Mauer man and Tautavel man.

We know just as little of what might have happened during the Riss Glaciation. Let us note, by the way, that geologists do not agree completely on the number, duration, and temperature of glacial periods. Let us just assume, then, that life continued during the Mindel and Riss Glaciations, and look at the evidence we have from the intervals of gentler climate, between the Mindel and Riss Glaciations and then between the Riss and Würm Glaciations.

The climate hardly differs from ours, with colder variations spaced over thousands of years (except, of course, during the Riss Glaciation, when the temperature was much lower). The landscape is still approximately the one that we have tried to imagine in the preceding chapter: oak, beech, hazelnut, and box-wood trees in wooded limestone areas or wild grapevine on sunny slopes. The animals still include some species extinct today, such as *Elephas antiquus* and the Merck rhinoceros; but as a whole, the fauna is already ours: deer, beaver, wild horse, and aurochs.

The life of archanthropians and paleoanthropians

It has been barely a generation since paleoethnological research (the study of the life of ancient man) has developed, along with excavation practices adapted to it. It is not that researchers of preceding generations were not motivated by the desire to know the details of prehistoric man's life, rather that most of them were interested in the most basic questions; they preferred stratigraphy, that is, sampling in vertical cross sections, allowing for the recovery of objects in chronological order, with the most ancient at the bottom.

This method limits information by reducing it to objects, correctly placed in chronological order but lacking almost entirely any other information. Objects were named according to their supposed function: scraper, borer, polisher, punch, awl, spear thrower . . . Even if we did not completely believe in the accuracy of the name, it stuck to the object.

The present method consists in retrieving by careful excavation not only objects, but all evidence preserved in its

In this deep part of one of Arcy's caves, the floor on which the Mousterians lived stayed intact. In the midst of rubble, we found the broken bones of horses and reindeer and flint tools abandoned tens of thousands of years ago by paleoanthropian hunters. (Photograph A. Leroi-Gourhan)

original context. A hearth, even if all its charcoal was collected to determine the woods used and to do an analysis of radiocarbon for dating purposes, is far more interesting if all the associated artifacts are left in their place, much as the man who lit the fire saw them. Excavations that proceed horizontally, leaving the remains in place so that they might be recorded through photographs, drawings, and latex molding, reveal the relationships among the remains before the context is destroyed in order to study the individual evidence (tools, fauna, flora, climate, human remains).

Data on the life of paleoanthropians or archanthropians

are still embryonic: On-site observations in a few places give us a chance to judge the usefulness and difficulties of this new method. The author has personal experience only in the methods he used at the Cave of the Hyena and the Cave of the Reindeer at Arcy-sur-Cure.

Cave of the Hyena. The layer contemporary with the jaw of Augustine was covered by eight layers of strata with Mousterian tools, and we excavated them centimeter by centimeter, trying to save even the most modest clues.

We took away, in small fragments (sometimes only a tooth), the remains of six or seven individuals: at least two adults and several children or adolescents. The cave they inhabited was dark, humid, crossed by a sort of trail leading to galleries several hundred meters long. In the intervals when no men lived there, they were replaced by bears, which came to sleep and, sometimes, to die.

Hyenas moved about the galleries, devouring cadavers of bears and the garbage of men; their excrement, which fossilizes perfectly, was found to have a wealth of bony matter. It was found in a layer twenty centimeters deep along the length of the path and several centimeters deep in the remainder of the cave.

In summer, Augustine and her family must have preferred to camp outside in the open air; but in winter they came back to their cave, amidst the excrement and carcasses, particularly the remains of the old hyenas, which had ended their existence on the same grounds as their banquets. Augustine and her family settled in the middle of the cave, simply pushing aside the most cumbersome bones. We did not find a preserved hearth, but here and there were stones reddened by fire and very small fragments of burned bones.

It is exceedingly rare to find an intact floor such as the one in the preceding illustration; ordinarily remains are covered with earth and distributed throughout several layers. Here is a cross section at Arcy, showing layers 16 to 20. Layer 20 is the level on which Augustine lived. The bones were cleaned of clay and the dust of fossilized hyena droppings. These are the debris of meals that included horses, aurochs, reindeer, sometimes chamois or deer. There are remains of wolves and hyenas as well. This photograph was taken some time before the discovery of Augustine, who is still a meter north, but another human maxillary was to be discovered two days later, ten centimeters behind the lower part of the vertical ruler. (Photograph A. Leroi-Gourhan)

These men must have eaten a lot of plant shoots, roots, and fruit; their teeth show heavy chewing. But they were also hunters of oxen and horses and rather deft butchers. They dismembered the dead animals at the kill site and hauled the big pieces to the cave, abandoning the remainder of the carcasses. All that was taken along was eaten, the bones scraped and then broken to extract the marrow. The remains were casually thrown behind them toward the cave walls. Thus, around this kind of central feeding place, a thick accumulation of animal remains formed, primarily horse and aurochs but including also reindeer and mammoths, which returned to the region with the coming of the Würm Glaciation. In this domestic garbage we find, from time to time, human remains, also broken. Does this testify to cannibalistic practices? It is difficult to say, but after all, it would be a sign of humanity, since men are the only primates who eat one another rather easily.

During the cold season plant food became rare and meat, too, was sometimes lacking. We can thus imagine these men with their low foreheads and powerful snouts entrenched in their leaking room, squatting in the refuse of hyenas, scraping and gnawing at their horse carcasses. One of these men had teeth so badly worn that all the front teeth were down to the gums and a series of abscesses had deeply pitted the bone.

The people of Arcy seem to have been true wild men, even for this period. Their way of chipping flint, although they used the correct techniques, was very crude. The western and oriental paleoanthropians, with their bigger skulls, were no doubt more evolved. But no one's customs were marked by excessive gentleness. The Fontéchevade man

seems to have died of a severe blow to the top of his skull;
the one from Steinheim suffered from a blow that deprived
him of a good quarter of his face, and both skulls were found
mixed, in suspicious fashion, with cooking remains.

Acheulian industry

We stopped in the preceding chapter at the time when the
hammer stone, hitting the flint at right angles, strikes off
Clactonian flakes and produced choppers and rudimentary
bifaces. The tools made this way were heavy, with an irregular cutting edge. From the beginning of the new period, flint
knappers (workers) can be divided into three groups:

-those who lag behind in the old method of perpendicular
 blows, hardly modifying them (Fontéchevade man)

-those who perfect the techniques in regions where flint
 is abundant and found in rather large nuggets of good
 quality

-those who are reduced to having their creative imagination work on small, poor, scarce, or difficult rocks

So progress is affected by complex factors. It varies according to the technical level, which may differ from one
group to the other, and according to the unequal quality of
raw materials, which goes from big flint nodules weighing
several kilos to chert, a sort of opaque flint that breaks poorly
and that is found only in small pieces.

Let us begin our study under the best conditions: with the
products of the Acheulians of the Somme and Seine-Mari-
time regions of northern France. A large part of these artifacts were found at Saint-Acheul, therefore this tool
assemblage and the culture whose remains it represents were
named for the town.

Let's take a sizable nodule, flat and oval, and instead of brutally hammering it on its flat surface, let's give it a sharp blow on the edge. A flatter and longer flake than the Clactonian results. Let's continue the strokes along the edge, alternately on each face. We get a flat biface with an irregular edge and extensively worked surfaces. We can remove the irregularities of the cutting edge with smaller hammer blows. Finally we have a beautiful almond-shaped flint with a straight cutting edge, which is both efficient and balanced.

We could have begun by preparing the flint nodule in the Clactonian manner, before removing the long flakes from the edge with the same stone hammer. To finish the piece and make it flatter, we could have hit it along its edge with a hard wooden stick. At this point we would have reached the high point of the Acheulian technique, creating the magnificent flint "limandes" found in regions where the stone is particularly fine.

Considered from the point of view of progress, the technique we have just described has great significance. Instead of only a limited number of moves, several successive series of steps form an already complicated chain:

-choosing a suitable flint nodule, keeping in mind the form of the tool to be manufactured

-preparing the nucleus, using Clactonian procedures

-removing flatter and longer chips along the edge (new procedure) to bring the piece to a state of prefinishing

-using a wooden hammer (new procedure and tool), to make the flint tool very flat and perfectly shaped.

Such a sequence shows true intelligence in the most human sense, even if thousands of years were necessary for it to be established and even if the successive workers were not conscious of the change.

The Acheulian blows are less angled than the Clactonian, and the production of the biface becomes much more precise.

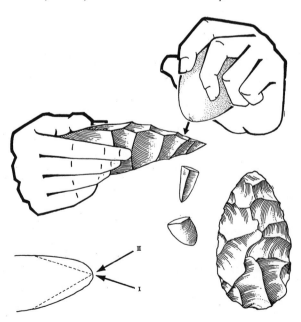

The Acheulian biface, with long flakes struck off and fine retouching on the edges, acquired a highly regular form and a greater effectiveness than those of the Abbevillian biface.

It is easy to see the reasons in this evolution. The first is technical: The new cutting edge is superior to the old one and the good Acheulian limande is a very efficient tool. The other reason is economic: With a kilo of flint, Clactonian or Abbevillian man manufactures a rudimentary biface endowed with ten centimeters of wavy cutting edge; while with the same weight in flint, the Acheulian worker manufactures two limandes, each of which has twenty centimeters of good cutting edge. Flint quarries are not found everywhere and cutting edges are used up rather quickly; the Acheulian hunter thus has freedom of movement four times that of his predecessors. From oldest times, problems of economic geography are very important; we shall see that all human evolution has had as a principal motive the freeing of men from their sources of raw material.

Triangular points and Levallois flakes

Despite progress, the biface remains heavy and cumbersome. It has the qualities and the faults of an all-purpose tool; it cuts, punctures, scrapes, it digs the soil if necessary, it does everything, but nothing perfectly. It takes a long time to manufacture. Before the biface even reached its highest point, man found something much better.

This time let's take a good flint core weighing several kilos. We'll peel it with great Clactonian blows to take off the crust and prepare good striking surfaces. By combining the Clactonian technique with the Acheulian removal of long flakes, we can make a type of core characterized by great ribs all around. The block is ready for the manufacture of a new tool. Let's take off several small flakes to prepare ourselves a very narrow striking platform. We'll strike a good blow near the edge: A small flake comes off that takes along a part of the rib. Another stronger blow farther in produces a *triangular point*, ten or fifteen centimeters long, with an excellent edge. The point is reinforced at the end by the rib; its cutting edges are sharper than the biface; its base is thin and flat and it can be attached to a shaft for use as a knife as well as a spear point.

From one kilo of raw material we can manufacture, on the average, ten points, that is, two meters of cutting edge. With five or six kilos of points prepared in advance, a hunter could be at peace for at least several months; he could go one hundred kilometers from home and seek the Merck rhinoceros in the best grazing grounds.

But hold on! The nucleus of these points still remains. It has taken on, more or less, the shape and volume of a box turtle shell. If we prepare a good striking surface at the best end and give a last blow (very difficult to estimate well), we come out with a magnificent flint leaf, flat and as long as a hand, with sharp, narrow cutting edges. This is a *Levallois flake*. We'll keep it safe in a fold of our garment, made of a giant bearskin. It may serve all kinds of uses. We can use it, as is, to cut; we could also, after finely retouching the edges, transform it into a very elegant biface.

We have just lingered in a region where flint abounds in great blocks. But in other regions where there is a lot of game, flint exists only in the form of nodules hardly as big as two fists. Here mass manufacture becomes a problem. Let's take one of these discouraging flint nodules, prepare it as a "turtle shell" (a very small turtle). We'll prepare the flatter surface either in a regular convex bulge or with several parallel ribs. Then we'll remove a Levallois flake across the top. From the convex version, we get a normal Levallois flake. With only one rib, we obtain a very satisfactory triangular flake (but only one per nucleus). With several ribs . . . but it would be better to stop here and wait a few thousand years, or we would anticipate the next chapter.

Thus a real technological revolution happened during the phase we call Moustero-Levalloisian (from the name of the cave of Le Moustier, in the Dordogne region, and Levallois-Perret, near Paris). Man plays freely with all the possibilities passed on from the preceding periods. Flint specialists variously use Clactonian technique, the preparation of the biface, and lateral flaking, with as much mastery and technical judgment as the good carpenter who chooses his wood, plays with its qualities and faults, estimates his hammer blows, and pressures, foresees, corrects, and coordinates his procedures.

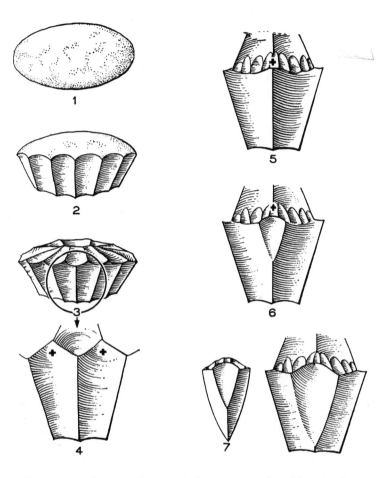

The steps in the manufacture of the "mass-produced" triangular point:

1. The raw flint nodule.
2. The edges are roughed out to make a series of regular ribs.
3. The top is prepared to make suitable striking platforms.
4. A close-up of a lateral rib, showing the hollow on top that must be chipped into a convex striking platform.
5. Retouching produces a useful striking platform.
6. First a small thinning flake is removed.
7. The second blow yields the finished point.

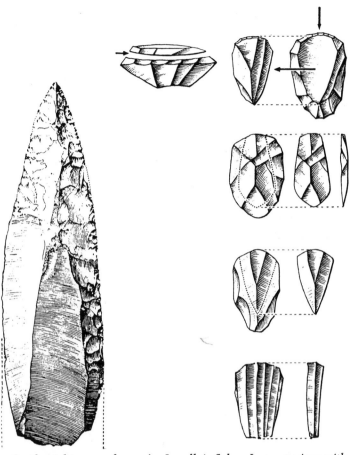

On the right are nucleuses for Levallois flakes. In comparison with the preceding illustration we can see that the preparation of the nodule is the same, but instead of taking flakes around the edge, they are removed laterally from the flat, broad top. Preparation of this top surface enables the maker to remove a triangular point, a large flake, or a blade.

To the left, a triangular point 21 centimeters long. We can see the thinning at the base and the very fine retouching that straightens the cutting edge and the point. Such large examples generally are rare because they were usually reworked into smaller tools when they broke down; but in regions where flint is found in large blocks, their manufacture must have been frequent, and we find thousands of points 8 to 15 centimeters long.

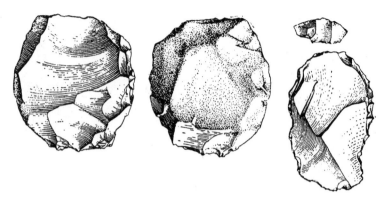

These artifacts were found near the remains of Augustine, exactly between the lower jaw and the bones on pg. 76. The two on the left are small nucleuses in the shape of a turtle shell; from one a large flake has been removed and the other a Levallois flake. Even in raw materials as difficult to work as a chert, the men of Arcy managed to manufacture their tools according to the most modern techniques of the period.

All this skill was acquired before the beginning of the Würm Glaciation, a time for which we possess remains of men whose physiques confound us still. Despite his primitive look and all we know about his rather crude life, the man of Arcy, as clumsy as he was, knew how to use the poor chert of the region to create points manufactured according to the technique of the little turtle shell. As for men of the northwest, where good flint was abundant, they delighted in refined and shapely points twenty centimeters long.

In reality, when we look at the most beautiful flints manufactured during this period, we feel that a sense of art has begun its evolution. We possess no artwork from the time; if any had existed, it would have been lost. But we are already in the presence of what one calls functional esthetics, that is, the search in the manufacture of tools for the most beautiful and efficient forms.

7

The Last Primitives

It is remarkable how much progress had been made before the Würm Glaciation began. Forty to eighty thousand years will still elapse until our modern period, and yet three-quarters of human time has already gone by. Although there is still no written history, what we shall now see is much clearer than what went before. Before the Würm Glaciation, caves were invaded by water many, many times, so that we can count on the fingers of one hand the earlier ones that remained intact. Starting with the Würm Glaciation, on the other hand, the caves will be filled with remains that have lasted until our time.

During the first part of the glaciation, France is peopled by those strange beings called Neanderthals. More advanced men already existed, but they probably lived more to the south, perhaps in the Near East. The climate of those regions was temperate then, and what is today's desert was covered with vegetation. In Palestine, remains of paleoanthropians were discovered who were very close to the neanthropians. But our western European regions, with their cold and humid climate, were probably abandoned by the more evolved humans of the period. During the next several millennia, our hunting grounds will be trod by the Neanderthals, the last representatives of the paleoanthropians.

At Arcy-sur-Cure we found more than a dozen archeological deposits for this Würm period. Thus we have a general idea of how this period evolved. The Würm Glaciation was not uniformly cold; several times the temperature rose, only to fall again.

First scene: It is still rather mild. The landscape is that of present-day France (except for the lack of agriculture, of course). There are many wild horses and aurochs, some fallow deer and boar. Augustine and her family settle down and live in the cave, in the way we have described.

Second scene: There is an intense cold spell, which lasts for three layers and decreases little by little. A lot of reindeer, some horses, chamois, which sought refuge in the low regions, and polar foxes. Mousterian culture gradually takes root.

Third scene: The cold is less biting. Still reindeer, but horses are now numerous and boar appear here and there. The climate is rather dry.

Fourth scene: It rains. Everything streams down, everything thaws. Mud washes through fissures in the ceiling of the cave and covers all the preceding layers with a heavy coat. Only some hyenas risk coming. Man is elsewhere, in drier places.

Fifth scene: The forest has returned. The weather is agreeable. Reindeer are rarer. Herds of horses and aurochs are common. Small wild donkeys have come up from the south with large deer and boar. The culture is not altogether the same; men work with wood; we know it from the numerous small, thick, flint scrapers they abandoned. They hunt with bolas. They still keep the tool kit of the Mousterian

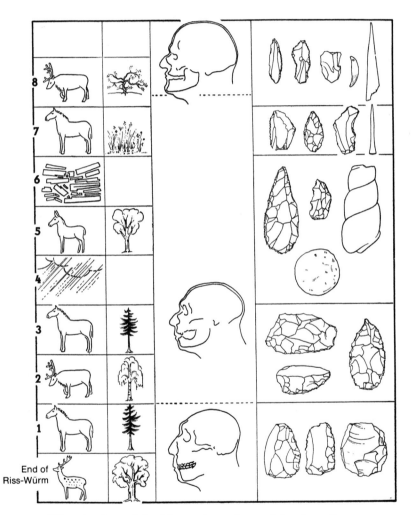

Climatic chart of the Mousterian culture of the Arcy Caves.

period, but add to it some tools we find still later on in the hands of *Homo sapiens,* such as carinated scrapers and burins. Even better, they collect curios, which is a signal of the emergence of art. This is the last bloom of paleoanthropic culture; they are doubtless influenced by the art and the techniques of *Homo sapiens* groups, which have settled not far from the region.

Sixth scene: Confusion reigns. Is it an effect of climatic changes and thawing, or the result of sudden activity of the Auvergne volcanoes? The cave ceilings fall in, solidly sealing the old layers of the soil. This sounds the death knell of the great Mousterian culture.

Seventh scene: The last primitives have come back to seek shelter from the bad weather, settling on the debris of the fallen cave entrances. They seem uprooted, their industry is wretched. They collect their ancestors' flints to chip anew and they manufacture their tools from poor rocks found nearby. The cold returns.

Eighth scene: The weather is extremely cold. Reindeer reappear with polar foxes. But a new culture is being born: that of the Reindeer Age, which we shall find again in the next chapter.

At Arcy, we have no human remains for the third, fourth, fifth, and sixth stages; but in some fifty other caves in France and western Europe, remains of Neanderthal men have been found in the corresponding periods. The Cave of Arcy has yielded, on the other hand, some few remains of the men of the seventh and eighth stages, those who saw the ceilings collapse and culture change completely. A rather extraordinary fact—these men were still paleoanthropians, but we do not know enough of them to say that they still completely resembled Neanderthals.

The life of the Neanderthals

France was peopled by Neanderthals during a long period, comprising the second, third, fourth, and fifth stages of the caves at Arcy. The climate was humid, in general rather cold, getting milder toward the end. The population must have been relatively dense, judging by the hundreds of thousands of flint tools left behind in nearly all regions. It is true that the zones where one finds skeletons are much smaller: But that is because the bones only resisted time in the limestone regions, where there are caves.

In every place where we find human fossils dating from this period, they are Neanderthal, and their tools are Mousterian. There are, however, certain nuances from one region to another and, probably, from one period to another; through the successive layers of Arcy-sur-Cure, we can follow the regular evolution of Mousterian culture.

Neanderthals are still paleonthropians, that is, beings whom one almost hesitates to consider as true men, so little appealing is their physical appearance. Yet we saw that their technical capabilities are fully human. In any case, long before them, men who knapped flint already knew how to transmit the skill of their craft, and with a stone block in their hands, they thought exactly as any man thinks who creates something. The next question that can be raised about the Neanderthal is whether he was aware of religion or art. The least spark in these two areas would bring him closer to us. According to our personal convictions, we want to think that primitives were gradually led to construct beliefs to protect them against the fear of death, or else to believe that they participated to some degree in divine revelation. Beliefs of either sort would endow these beings with their share of humanity.

While our data on the religious and artistic life of Neanderthals are few, they are nevertheless precise. The skeleton of La Chapelle-aux-Saints lay in a grave that had been dug to bury it. The adolescent whose remains were found in Le Moustier was also buried, and, in La Ferrassie, several burials were exhumed, which had been arranged with particularly well-crafted flint offerings. At Arcy-sur-Cure, we saw that poor Augustine, far from having been buried, had probably been the object of a farewell banquet, but this act of cannibalism belongs to the old period. In the layer corresponding to the relatively mild period that preceded the Reindeer Age at Arcy-sur-Cure we recovered a grave with the remains of a body, unfortunately almost completely decomposed.

In brief, Neanderthals (at least those who immediately preceded the Reindeer Age) buried their dead; even sometimes, as at La Ferrassie, they surrounded the burial with ceremony. We also saw that they collected unusual stones or fossil shells gathered during excursions, so we can surmise that the beginnings of symbolic human thinking date from this period.

Another fascinating problem is that of the origin of language. When did men begin to communicate by speech?

We can hold as certain that language already existed, at least in a rudimentary form, among anthropians whom we know from the Clacto-Abbevillian tool industry. And beyond that, their interest in the dead must have made use of an even richer language. Their brain, larger than ours, was perhaps differently organized in certain areas, but it allowed, like ours, the use of language. The shape of the face and the markings of the muscles of the tongue, on the other hand, give the impression that mimicry and the movements for

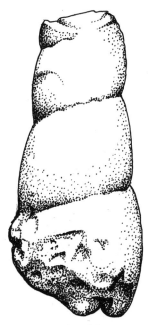

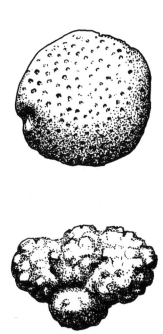

One of the oldest amateur collections known. It consists of (left) a fossil of a big shell from the Secondary Period, 225 to 70 million years ago, (bottom right) a coral of the same period, and a rounded piece of iron pyrite. They were found in final Mousterian layers in the midst of flint tools and animal bones. These curios were gathered rather far from the caves where the paleoanthropians lived and brought home by them.

speech were more rudimentary than in contemporary humanity.

We may assume that Neanderthals knew the basic unit of social life: the family. But beyond it, how were they organized? Did they live in bands, or in tribes? Did they recognize family groups and chiefs? The answer to these questions is not recorded in the book of the earth. All we can do is to apply to Neanderthals the universally valid rule that, for people who live by hunting, the size of the social group is proportional to the abundance of game on the territory available to the hunters. Practically speaking, this means that Neanderthal groups rarely went beyond a few individuals, though several groups might unite to hunt migrating game.

No people living today can be compared to the Neanderthal. Yet the Australian aborigines and those of Tierra del Fuego still could, half-a-century ago, give us a fairly good picture of their life. This is especially true for the inhabitants of Tierra del Fuego, whose climate, at the southernmost tip of the South American continent, was rather similar to that which must have prevailed in Europe at the beginning of the Würm Glaciation: cold and humid.

The Fuegians still lived, a few years ago, in little groups of a few families, just large enough to feed themselves without going beyond the resources of their hunting territory. The main part of their food was acquired by hunting and fishing, but in order to bear the periods of famine, they must have depended on the food resources provided by wild plants and small animals, even insects. They lived in rounded huts built with branches and brush and huddled around a small hearth, fed as much as possible by pieces of broken bones. They had great resistance to cold: They wore only a square piece of skin slung across their backs, just big enough to cover them when they squatted, their backs turned against the wind. Their domestic implements were reduced to the minimum: baskets woven in the simplest manner, harpoons with stone points, rocks used as hammers or pounders, thick end-scrapers, and knives. It is impossible

With differences in a few details, this group of Australians gives us a picture of what an encampment of paleoanthropians could have been. The hut of branches, the wooden weapons, some baskets that Neanderthal man perhaps already knew how to manufacture, a few flint tools, and these entirely nude men around the hearth, on a soil strewn with debris, give a good picture of an encampment of Mousterian times. (Collection Musée de l'Homme)

to find in the recent world a clearer example of what the Neanderthal mode of life must have been.

As far as the technology of the Neanderthals, it is not necessary to invoke other peoples. Prehistoric sites have provided enough samples of artifacts to allow us to make a precise account.

We left off, in the preceding chapter, with the Moustero-Levalloisian technical revolution. Now that they know how to knap small flint blocks, our hunters are no longer obliged to stay close to the quarries. An occasional expedition to bring back a few kilos of raw material is enough. This they transform into tools for all purposes: triangular points and scrapers.

The inhabitants of the Arcy-sur-Cure Cave were precisely at this stage in our first scene. Augustine's husband rather economically chipped the small blocks to make triangular points and scrapers, using the waste and the rest of the core for other purposes.

His successors inherited the tradition, and during the second and third scenes (very, or somewhat, cold), they continue to knap flint with an average yield of two meters of cutting edge per kilo. But these successors are either less lazy or better informed: Instead of using the pebbles of the Cure River and the poor chert of the cliff, they look for good flint at least thirty kilometers from the caves. Their production rises. We also note that their technology is more varied: Along with points and scrapers, we find end-scrapers and notched tools, which show us that they carefully scraped the shafts of their weapons. This is the indirect evidence of spears and javelins that, because they were of wood, have disappeared.

Then the very rainy period of the fourth scene arrives. The milder temperature brings back red deer and boar to the region. It also seems that it attracts different kinds of men to the north. At any rate, Augustine's descendants have been in contact with a new culture. It is no longer Mousterian; it is not yet that of the Reindeer Age. We are in a muddled, intermediary period. It seems to have become difficult to reach the flint quarries on the other side of the great forest, for men saved their raw material, chipping and rechipping the old tools, which sometimes ended by being

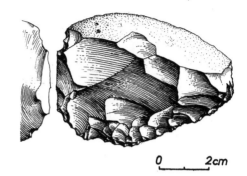

The two most used tools of the Mousterian. The triangular point (left) could serve as a knife or javelin point. The side-scraper perhaps served to scrape skins, but it seems more likely to have been a kind of domestic knife to skin game, cut meat, and do the thousand tasks that demanded a cutting edge.

as small as a fingernail. The good quality flint is reserved for the points of weapons. Side-scrapers, end-scrapers, and the first burins (a chisellike tool) are manufactured from chert and common pebbles. The technique is still that of the Moustero-Levalloisian industry. Tools are thick, large, and still yield approximately two meters of cutting edge per kilo. But progress shows in the fact that the tools are much more varied: points, side-scrapers, thick end-scrapers, burins, and the first backed knives. These tools indicate that woodworking is becoming more and more important.

Besides tools in chipped stone, we frequently encounter stone balls of sandstone or limestone, shaped by hammering. They were probably attached in pairs to thongs and were thrown to hit and lasso game, like the cowboys of today do in southern Argentina.

We are now very close to the Age of the Reindeer. On

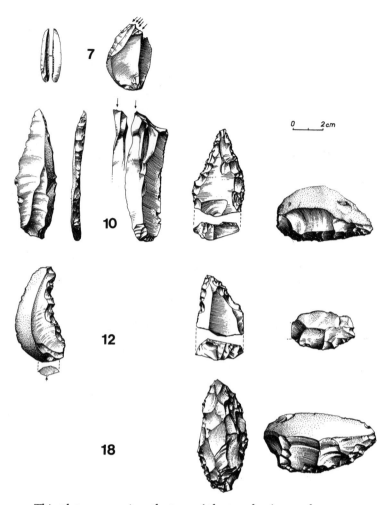

This plate summarizes the tens of thousands of years that separate the Mousterian culture from the Reindeer Age. These are tools placed in the chronological order in which they were found in the ground. On the right, the Mousterian flake tools: side-scraper and triangular point. On the left, the Upper Paleolithic blade tools: the burin and backed blade. Layer 18 corresponds to the high point of the Mousterian culture. Layers 12 and 10 represent the transition between flake industries and blade industries. We see that there is a true transition in 12: We find a blade with natural back made on a flake, while during the Early Perigordian in 10, the backed knife is made from a blade, but we still find the earlier point and side-scraper made from flakes. Layer 7 is from the Gravettian culture.

the large scene of prehistory, the last actor, our fellow man, makes his appearance: *Homo sapiens sapiens,* in English the man of wisdom of the wisdoms (as he was willing to call himself), with the high forehead and the skillful paintbrush, who will begin to decorate cave walls.

8

The Reindeer Age

Homo sapiens sapiens, that is, our fellow man, appears in Europe during the second part of the Würm Glaciation, where he will develop the culture of the Reindeer Age. Specialists place the beginnings of this event about 40,000 years before our era. Great progress in the chronology of the period has been made during the past few years. By measuring the radioactive carbon of charcoal and bones discovered in archeological deposits, relatively precise dates have been established. It would appear that the end of Mousterian begins about 50,000 years before our era. The transition to the Perigordian lasted until approximately 30,000 years ago; the Aurignacian corresponds to about the same period. The Solutrean age was approximately 18,000 years ago and the Magdalenian lasted from about 15,000 to 9,000 years before our era. Thanks to this scientific dating method, the absence of writing is not so crucial, and we can almost say that the limits of historical times have receded 50,000 years.

Here is the first certain date in all of humanity's history. It means that the Age of the Reindeer lasted at least thirty thousand years, and that ten thousand years more elapsed between the end of the Reindeer Age and the modern era.

After the period of cold and humidity that tested Neanderthal man, the climate became somewhat milder. Then,
during the second part of the Würm Glaciation, it became
dry and very cold. Again we find the game of earlier periods—that is, wild horses and aurochs—but reindeer, this
time, clearly predominate. There are also bison, mammoths,
woolly rhinoceroses, ibex, and, in the French southwest, the
curious saiga antelope, an animal of the cold steppes of
eastern Europe and central Asia. The carnivores are found
in abundance, especially the wolf, the usual predatory companions of reindeer herds.

The landscape, during the extremely cold peaks, resembled that of contemporary Siberia, with giant glaciers covering the Alps and the Pyrenees. Zones of lichened tundra
alternated with a marshy taiga spread with small birch and
pine trees. Dry continental winds brought the steppe into
regions far from the glaciers. The forest maintained itself in
protected spots along waterways. Such a climate favors large
game, and the streams, nourished by the melting of glaciers,
were perfect for the development of salmon and trout; so
that far from hindering the settlement of man, the climate
of the last part of the Würm Glaciation should have offered
abundant resources in game and fish.

In France, human remains prior to the Reindeer Age are
those of paleoanthropians, particularly Neanderthals. This
does not imply that men similar to modern men did not live
in other parts of the world, even though paleoanthropians
still peopled western Europe, but the humid cold and thick
forest perhaps held them back. The deep forest is not the
favorite habitat of hunters because game density is low. We
can suppose then that, after a short period of mild weather,

the climate again became colder and also drier. The paleoanthropians who still lived in our regions saw the coming of
large herds of reindeer and hunters of a more developed
human type who followed them.

We do not know what the first contacts between the
ancient humanity and the new one were. What is certain is
that from this moment on Neanderthal man definitely
disappears.

Homo sapiens sapiens

Although they were very different from the paleoanthropians, the newcomers were not all exactly alike either.

Right from the beginning of the Reindeer Age, there
lived in France men like the one whose skull was discovered
in the Cro-Magnon Cave at Les Eyzies in the Dordogne
region. They were tall (approximately 1.8 meters) with an
elongated skull and a short face. Two or three other speci-
mens of this "race of Cro-Magnon" were found in the
Dordogne and near Monaco on the Mediterranean.

There have also been discoveries of some ten other creatures from the same period, close to Cro-Magnon man, yet
different. Some are tall, others average; some had a slightly
less elongated skull. This shows that Cro-Magnon man did
not live everywhere and that, from one region to another,
human types were already varied, just as they are today.

Finds were made in Europe of the remains of some one
hundred men of the Reindeer Age (or Upper Paleolithic);
those of the Chatelperronian (35,000 before our era), still
poorly known, appear still to have Neanderthal traits (Arcy,
Saint-Césaire). Then come those of the Aurignacian (30,000
years ago) and the time that follows, until the end of the

Upper Paleolithic, that is, the final Magdalenian (about 9,000 years ago). Different human types followed one another over the millennia. The best known is that of Cro-Magnon, who represents a radical break with all the types that preceded him: high skull vault, thin brow ridges, rectangular eye sockets, relatively narrow nose, well-delineated canine depressions, well-developed chin.

It is difficult to tell the race of fossil men. The only research can be an analysis of cranial characteristics, but it seems that the oldest subjects are already somewhat related in their form to present-day races. The differences among races could very well go back quite far into the past. Most of the examples of skulls allow us to think that the great racial masses each dominated a continent, but it is more difficult to tell whether the early archanthropians *(Homo erectus)* already showed these racial differences. The presence of remains of *Homo erectus* in the whole of the Old World and the many variations of *Pithecanthropus, Sinanthropus, Atlanthropus* seem at least to allow a tentative hypothesis of early racial distributions.

To summarize, Europe, and in particular France, was peopled during the Upper Paleolithic by men slightly different from one another, a bit different from today's races, but already so close to Europeans that one may consider them as the true beginning of modern European humanity.

Flint blades

Prehistorians distinguish several cultural trends for the Age of the Reindeer or Upper Paleolithic.

The Chatelperronian has already been mentioned. It forms a true transition period between the Mousterian (from Le Moustier in the Dordogne) and the Upper Paleo-lithic, and, as is usual during periods of cultural mutation, the main technological artifacts are borrowings from both cultures: Chatelperronian points and small side scrapers made from waste flakes.

The Aurignacian (Aurignac, in southwestern France)—30,000 years ago. Widely distributed in Western Europe, corresponds to Cro-Magnon man. Beginning of abstract figurative art.

The Gravettian (La Gravette, Dordogne region)—25,000 years ago. Part of the Perigordian culture.

The Solutrean (Solutré, southeastern France)—18,000 years ago. Characterized by flint points in the form of laurel leaves.

The Magdalenian (La Madeleine, Dordogne region)—from 15,000 to 9,000 years ago. Last phase of the Upper Paleolithic. Disappearance of the mammoth, rhinoceros, and reindeer.

The Epipaleolithic represents the transition to the Meso-lithic.

Let's first examine the common character of these diverse cultures, and then the particular characteristics that led to their separate classification.

You may recall that, at the end of Chapter 6, we were holding in our left hand a flint nucleus prepared by the removal of several parallel flakes across the top. Let's again pursue our unfinished procedure: Let us strike the nucleus on its side to produce several flakes, much longer than wide, and with parallel edges, not points. These flakes are blades, and from the day when it was possible to produce them, the living conditions of hunters were profoundly changed.

With a kilo of raw material, the Mousterian flint knappers could make two meters of cutting edge, an increased yield that allowed men to roam for long months without returning to the flint quarries. With the production of blades, men of the Age of the Reindeer made a considerable leap: six to eight meters of cutting edge per kilo for large blades, up to twenty or twenty-five meters for slim blades and bladelets. To this must be added rejects, preparatory flakes, and broken flakes, which could still be used, depending on their form, for a large number of specialized tools. The freedom from flint sources becomes practically complete: Whether directly or by exchange, hunters can supply themselves with the minimum quantity of raw materials necessary to manufacture their weapons and tools.

To illustrate the importance of this technological revolution, let's go back a little in time. During the time of the Acheulian industry, man remains bound to regions where he could find flint or a good raw material substitute; a map recording places where Acheulian objects were found is more or less empty for regions where there is no stone for tools. In the period of the Moustero-Levalloisian industry, the distribution expands; flint tools, on the map, go beyond regions where stone is found; but there still remain extensive blank spaces and often, in regions far away from flint, only the most important weapons are manufactured in this precious raw material, the rest made the best way possible, with rocks of second-rate quality. During the Reindeer Age the empty spaces are filled on the map: Man from then on goes everywhere and he even abandons used tools made of good flint.

Should we conclude that the manufacture of blades was

discovered by *Homo sapiens?* Blades really are only a later development of earlier techniques, and it is possible that the first worker who practiced it was still a paleoanthropian. But it is indeed *Homo sapiens* who appear to have spread the new industry. Whenever we find blades, we can usually say that those who manufactured them were men similar to contemporary man. The trait most characteristic of Reindeer Age industry is the general use of flint blades as a point of departure for numerous tools. These blades are retouched: shaped to serve now as knives, now as end-scrapers, as borers, as burins.

Each period developed its type of tool, which we shall find again below. But two of them are common to the whole Age of the Reindeer: burins and scrapers.

The burin appeared long before the Age of the Reindeer, as early as the Acheulian industry, but only occasionally; toward the end of the Moustero-Levalloisian, the burin became more frequent, and from the beginning of manufacture into blades, it became very abundant. It was made by giving one or two blows to the end of the blade, so as to produce a little transverse cutting edge, similar to that of a modern chisel. It was the best tool for fashioning bone or antler; its abundance during the Age of the Reindeer corresponds to increased bone working, especially that of antler.

The end-scraper, too, already existed before the Age of the Reindeer, but in smaller quantities. We are not certain of its use, but hunters probably used it to scrape skins, as Eskimos and Fuegians did during the last century.

In fact, the industry of chipped flint, endlessly perfected since the first Clactonian flake, attains its peak during the Age of the Reindeer. No important innovation will be brought to it afterward, with the possible exception, at the

FOR A KILOGRAM
OF FLINT

The Abbevillian produces 10
centimeters of useful cutting edge

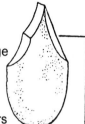

10 centimeters

The Acheulian produces—

40 centimeters

The Mousterian produces—

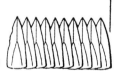

2 meters

The Magdalenian produces—

6–20 meters

The first "economic statistic" of human history shows that, from the beginning of technology, raw material and the conditions of transport have influenced manufacture.

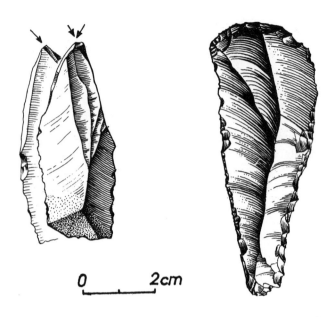

The burin (left) and the end-scraper are tools common to the whole of the Upper Paleolithic. These are the tools for work on bone, ivory, and antler. We see at the end of the burin the small flakes that were removed to make a small working edge, pointed and extremely strong. (Don't forget, flint scratches steel.) The forms of burins are varied; this one is of a very common type. On the end-scraper we can see retouching at the tip to give rounded working edges, like certain planes used by carpenters.

beginning of the Bronze Age, of the manufacture of very long flint blades with an extraordinary finish, the ultimate marvel of the last stone manufacturers, who had to compete with the first molders of metal daggers.

Other raw materials: soft stone

During the Reindeer Age, flint and its replacements are not the only stones used. Soft stone is worked, just as bone and wood are worked, with flint burins. There are only a few dómestic objects in soft stone, but there are many engravings and sculptures on cave walls.

After the magnificent horses in bas-relief at Cap-Blanc in the southwest region and the fresco of various animals at Le Roc in southern France, the discovery was made at Angles-sur-l'Anglin in west-central France of a monumental fresco of bisons, horses, and ibexes, where the Magdalenian sculptor appears to be the equal of the finest artists of any age.

Wood

No wooden objects dating from the Age of the Reindeer have been preserved, but we have indirect evidence of their existence. At the end of the Mousterian, we already find notched tools and thin scrapers, most likely made to work wood or bone. Since we find almost no bone objects for the Mousterian, we are led to think that these tools were used to polish hafts of javelins, spears, and wooden sticks used to dig out edible roots.

During the Reindeer Age, we again find notched tools and thin scrapers, which must have been used for wood as well as for bone and antler. The existence of wooden objects is the more certain because thousands of javelin heads have been found with bevels for attachment to a shaft. The most common javelin is shafted by means of a double bevel; when a javelin was broken during the hunt, the hunters brought back the shaft and removed the piece of javelin remaining in it. This explains why one finds many more javelin bases than points. These recovered pieces were probably used as small wedges, to pry off sections of reindeer antler from the antler itself.

We see bisons or horses pierced by these weapons in some twenty paintings or engravings. One point, though, remains obscure: We do not know what men of the Reindeer Age used to fell a tree or saw a big branch. All their flint material is much too light for such work. It includes neither large wedges nor anything resembling an axe. If they worked on large wooden pieces, we still have to learn the way they went about it. However, there have been experiments attempting to cut saplings of more than ten centimeters in diameter with a scraper used like an axe.

Bone, antler, ivory

Until the Reindeer Age, these materials seem to have been seldom worked. From time to time we find antler cut into small pieces, a bone flake that perhaps functioned as an awl, but there is nothing comparable to the handsome flint industry that existed in the same period. The poverty of the bone industry is amazing when we think of the skill of Mousterian artisans and the abundance of bone at their disposal. Toward the end of the Mousterian, we find certain bone tools that are better defined, awls in particular, but it is at the beginning of the Reindeer Age that there appears a flood of new objects: javelin points in reindeer antler or mammoth ivory, bone awls, pierced teeth to be threaded as pendants, thinned-out ribs to serve as spatulas or polishers.

Hides

Through the traces that flint knives left on the joints of reindeer, we know that paleoanthropians skinned these animals. Therefore, they must have used the skins, but we do not know how they were used. Beginning with the Solutrean, not only do we see the same traces on the bones, but we also find many sewing needles of bone, very fine borers in bone or flint, and big mammoth bones, scarred in all directions by flint knives, that must have served as work tables for cutting up skin for clothing.

The presence of needles and awls proves that skins were sewn with threads or thongs. Perhaps plant fibers or bark

Two Magdalenian javelin points of reindeer antler. On the left, two views of the biconical. In the middle, two views of one with a simple bevel and groove (according to D. Sacchi), and, on the right, a bone awl from the beginning of the Upper Paleolithic era.

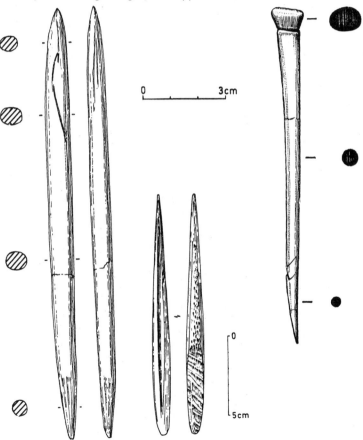

Male bisons urinate on the soil and roll in the mud to mark their territory. The above example is one of the famous "leaping" bisons of the Altamira Cave in Spain.

strips were used. Surely ibex or reindeer tendons were used also, for we often find the entire foot bones of these animals in the midst of tools (and not among food refuse). The foot may have served as a kind of spool to hold the tendon that was used as thread.

The skin of bears and hyenas may also have been used as rugs or blankets. On the earth floors inhabited during the Age of the Reindeer, we find toe joints and claws of these animals, broken at one end and marked by flint; they must have remained in the skins after someone had stripped the animal, just as in today's bedside rugs.

Minerals
Metal as such wasn't in use during the Reindeer Age. The only exception is the tons of red ochre (an iron oxide) used to decorate dwellings and graves. We sometimes also find pieces of natural iron, which must have been collected as

curios because of iron's density. On two occasions I found fragments of galena crystal as big as nuts in the levels of the Perigordian period. They were probably collected because of their metallic luster.

No pottery fragment has been identified with certainty in thousands of excavated sites. The few fragments of fired earth found were produced by the heat of hearths. These men who lived on the clay surfaces of caves do not seem to have known how to use this material to produce containers. There are, by the way, some recent peoples who did not use pottery (some Asiatic nomads, the American Indians, the Oceanians) and even others who, having possessed pottery, lost it for different reasons (such as the Ainu and the Eskimos of the North Pacific).

The great cultural trends:
The Chatelperronian or Early Perigordian
The men of the Reindeer Age belonged, as we saw, to different human types. Their cultures were not all the same either; variations on a common cultural base were developed in different periods and regions.

That which we call Perigordian (because numerous discoveries of it were made in the Perigord Caves) appeared soon after the intermediate period that followed the Mousterian. During the intermediate period men had not yet replaced flint flakes with blades, but they already manufactured burins, end-scrapers, and knives. The knives were made out of triangular flakes, one edge of which was cut straight across to give it a back, like one of our pocket knives. At the very beginning of the Perigordian, knives no longer appear to be made from flakes, but from blades. We call them "Chatelperronian points." At the same time, these tools have kept the arched backs of knives made from flakes. The tradition of curved backs will continue throughout the entire Reindeer Age, but gradually they will become thinner, their backs straighter, and they will be smaller.

At the beginning of the Perigordian, the Chatelperronian points and burins are almost the only signs of the appearance of a new industry. Then other tools with abrupt retouching on an edge appear. At the same time, the last traces of Mousterian industry disappear, and the influence of the Aurignacian trend (about which we shall speak below) brings new tools such as the carinated scraper.

Chatelperronian points. The Early Perigordian culture is character-
ized by this type of backed blade. We see on the curved back abrupt
retouching to make a knife blade with straight cutting edge and
blunt back.

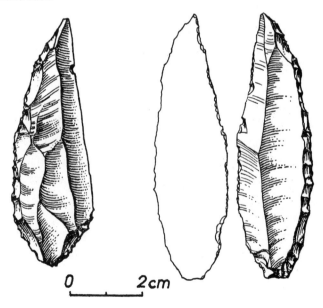

0 ___ 2cm

Two views of a carinated scraper. This is a very thick scraper found in Aurignacian layers.

During the Early Perigordian, bone objects are relatively scarce, but we already find awls and javelin points that are short and flat or cylindrical. The javelin points become progressively longer; during the Magdalenian they become blades whose length grows to thirty centimeters, and they are often highly decorated.

The Aurignacian
The Aurignacian is characterized by a very different method of flint knapping. Long and narrow chips are taken off in a row on thick pieces of flint (carinated scraper and busqued burin) and on long blades with two cutting edges. These two types of objects are also found in the Magdalenian in certain regions.

The bone industry primarily produced javelin points; they are short, flat, more or less diamond shaped, and split at the base.

The Perigordian and Aurignacian cultures flourished at the same time in a great part of their duration, so that, depending on the region, all possible combinations are found among their tools: Chatelperronian points and carinated scrapers, for example. This proves that our categories, such as the Perigordian and Aurignacian, correspond to technical trends rather than to groups of people having different traditions.

The Gravettian or Late Perigordian

This culture is characterized by a bladelet with a straight back, several centimeters long, and many special burins where the working edge is twisted. Engraving and painting become important at this time.

The Solutrean

The Solutrean is found primarily in southern France; it takes its name from Solutré and existed during the time between the Aurignacian and the Magdalenian cultures. Its characteristic tool is the "point in the form of a laurel leaf," which is the most beautiful flint object of the Reindeer Age. This point is made by flat retouching on the two faces, as were the small bifaces of the end of the Mousterian and some points of the beginning of the Perigordian; the Solutrean point represents, no doubt, the continuation of an old tradition, which Solutrean knappers brought from regions where the tradition was not broken.

The laurel leaf point is too thin to have been used at the end of a spear held in the hand; it could not have resisted the stresses of such a weapon. It could only reach its aim effectively if it were propelled with a great enough speed, such as with javelins or arrows. Wooden objects were not preserved and no engraving or painting shows us a bow. But it is possible that the bow and arrow already existed then.

On the other hand, there is positive evidence that another projectile weapon was used during the Reindeer Age, one that was used perhaps by Solutrean hunters, and that was definitely used by their Magdalenian successors. This weapon is the "spear thrower," a board or stick with a hook on the end on which is placed the heel of the javelin shaft. A rapid movement of the arm and wrist gives the javelin speed comparable to that of an arrow shot by a bow. This weapon was used most recently by the Eskimos, Australians, New Guineans, and the Native Americans of Peru, Mexico, and California.

The other objects of the Solutrean industry are not very different from those of the Late Aurignacian or Middle Magdalenian, except that the shape of certain tools is influenced by the flat retouching work characteristic of the laurel leaves.

Were the Solutreans, properly speaking, a people? Did they come from the south or the east and did they infiltrate themselves in the midst of Aurignacian groups? Or did the javelins with laurel leaf points simply represent a technological trend that diffused from tribe to tribe? The two hypotheses are not mutually exclusive. It is possible that a population practicing the Solutrean technique could have come from the outside and have settled for several centuries in certain parts of southwestern France, and that some already-settled populations adopted the fashion of the marvelous and fragile javelin.

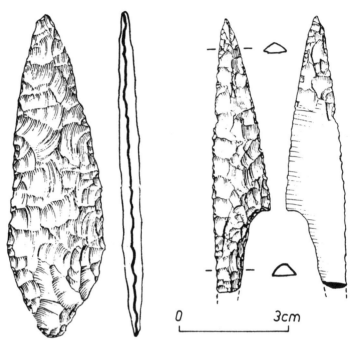

Two views of a Solutrean laurel leaf blade (left) and shouldered point (right). These points, long and flat, were attached to the end of javelin shafts. (From Ph. Smith)

The Magdalenian

At its beginning, the flint industry of the Magdalenian period differs little from the industries of the Aurignacian and Perigordian, which it directly succeeds where the people with Solutrean points did not appear. Later on, the Magdalenian evolves toward very small chipped stone tools, which leads progressively into the typical industry of the period following the Reindeer Age.

The bone and antler industry of the Magdalenian also continues that of preceding periods, but it develops further

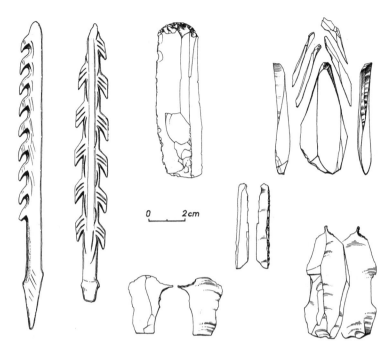

Magdalenian tool collection. Flint tools have decreased in size and are most often used for fine work on ivory and bone, and probably also on wood, bark, and leather. Clockwise from the left: two reindeer antler harpoons, one end-scraper made from a blade, one dihedral burin with waste bladelets that were removed during manufacture, two views of two microperforators and, in the center, a small backed blade.

Magdalenian pierced bâton. *These antler* bâtons *are probably levers to straighten antler javelin points by heating, which otherwise tended to revert to the natural curve of the antler.*

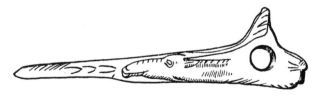

with a certain originality, producing notably "spear throwers" and perforated *bâtons*. These last objects are pieces of reindeer antler with a hole at one end the diameter of a thumb. Sometimes called a "scepter of leadership," they must have been used, with heat, to straighten javelin points. Javelin points manufactured from bladelets of antler followed the curved line of the antler. One could straighten them by heating them and by using the *bâton* with a hole as a lever. When we find these javelin points at excavations, most often they have returned to their original curved shape and would be unusable for hunting. Besides innumerable Magdalenian javelins, in certain regions we also find harpoons with one or two rows of barbs, which were probably used to capture big fish.

As the bone and antler industry developed to its peak, so did art develop fully in the Magdalenian period. In fact, for the whole of the Reindeer Age, the most impressive trait is the appearance of art and religion.

We had already assumed, among the last Neanderthal men, a rudimentary artistic or religious tendency, from the facts that collections of objects and some red ochre were present in their dwellings. But this bears no comparison to the testimony that *Homo sapiens* of the Reindeer Age left for us. Artistic activity began to develop from the middle of the Aurignacian period. The Solutrean, too, left some beautiful works, but a true blossoming of prehistoric art appears near the end of the Aurignacian and continues to the end of the Magdalenian. It is the great epoch of slabs engraved with animals and human figures, hundreds of decorated objects, dozens of caves whose walls are covered with paintings and engravings of animals and signs, and burials with funeral objects and ochre.

Toward the end of the Magdalenian, art became rapidly transformed. The walls of caves no longer show new figures, whether painted or engraved; the decoration of objects evolves toward simpler forms. Then the artistic flowering disappears completely at the end of the Würm Glaciation.

In a way, the settlement of *Homo sapiens* in these regions is a continuation of the development of a culture that probably had deep links to the Mousterian past. But its meaning is much more accessible to our ways of thinking when we carefully uncover the ancient surface where the hunters of the Reindeer Age lived; when we find the flat stones they laid down to level the floor; when we see a needle lost between two stones, a javelin that still bears the traces of the burin with which it was manufactured, the stone lamp with a trace of the wick still apparent on the charred edge. . . . Then these men, lost for fifteen or twenty thousand years, seem very near to us.

But what was their daily life like?

9

Life During the Reindeer Age

The life and customs of men of the Reindeer Age are far better known to us than those of their paleoanthropian predecessors. When we tried to revive Augustine, we had to be satisfied with little separate snapshots with no continuity. On the other hand, we are able to picture the life of *Homo sapiens* in the Reindeer Age more extensively.

Hunting and fishing
The weapons most used seem to have been spears, javelins, and harpoons. At any rate, we have sure proof of their existence, since flint and bone examples were preserved. Probably there were also wooden weapons, such as clubs and throwing sticks similar to the boomerang. But wooden objects have disappeared. In any case, they were of little use against big game. As almost everywhere among big-game hunters, before the invention of the gun, the javelin was the most important weapon, as it still was in the Middle Ages.

The javelins were very probably thrown with the help of a spear thrower; their points were made of ivory or reindeer antler, except among the Solutreans, who used flint points.

Harpoons appear rather late in the Magdalenian; they are javelins whose point detaches in the body of the animal; it is attached to a thong, which can be released if necessary to avoid snapping the point and which ensures holding on to the prey, just as with a fishing line. The harpoon is a weapon that was used only in water, for large fish or aquatic mammals; on earth the thong would surely break if it were pulled by a stronger animal. Perhaps several javelin points were attached in a cluster at the end of the shaft, to make a pronged fish-spear or trident.

It is more or less certain that men of the Reindeer Age knew how to trap animals. Like some American Indians or Lapps, they must have cornered herds of reindeer or horses and driven them into a ravine. Or, more simply, they pushed them into gorges to massacre them en masse. Perhaps they knew snares and nooses, but we have no proof. Certain drawings in caves were once believed to represent pits or traps made with timber to capture mammoths or bisons. But it is believed today that they are abstract geometric signs.

The use of tree trunks for lumber requires plenty of wood-cutting equipment, and, as we have indicated in the preceding chapter, no excavation has yielded such materials during the Reindeer Age.

Briefly, what we know with certainty is that the men of this period hunted with javelins. This was enough at any rate to insure a variety of game. But we can ask ourselves how they managed to master mammoths and rhinoceroses. The javelin (even when it is poisoned) is too light a weapon for the skin of these giants. Just as for the working of large pieces of wood, here too there is a prehistoric problem that has not been resolved.

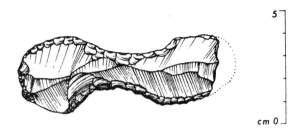

Above, a strangulated Aurignacian blade, used for the working of bone wands and javelin shafts.

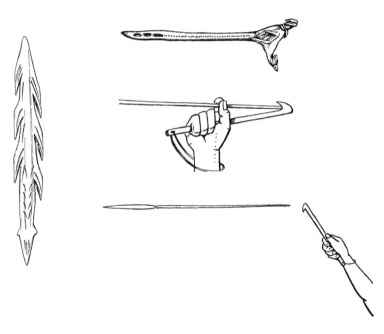

To the left, a Magdalenian harpoon. The harpoon, whose detachable head was attached to the shaft by a line, is a fishing weapon. We can suppose that Magdalenians used them to capture salmon and big trout. To the right, "spear thrower" and how it was used to cast javelins.

Many birds were also captured for food. We do not know by what means, but we think the methods were similar to those of the Eskimos: by hand, with a javelin, with a stone, perhaps even in a snare.

Food gathering

The gathering of fruit, seeds, shoots, and roots certainly played an important role in the activities of people of the Reindeer Age. Even among contemporary Eskimos, who live under much more unfavorable conditions, plant foods are important.

No evidence, not even indirect, remains of the food plants of the Reindeer Age people. We know the plants that were available thanks to fossil pollens of the period. The plants were those of the northern tundra-parkland: many berries (such as huckleberries), mushrooms, the interior bark of pine and birch trees in the forest areas, some plants with tubers or bulbs, such as wild lily, green shoots of grassy plants, young birch leaves. Plants could not possibly provide much in the way of food for winter; they were only important during summer months. Before the appearance of farming, these regions of France had only a few plant food species. It is only after the Reindeer Age that grain plants appeared, coming from the southeast and east. Long centuries would pass before edible roots like the carrot and turnip would become foods, more centuries yet for the bean and potato.

Thus we can imagine people of the Reindeer Age gathering plants to eat right away rather than storing them. Without game or fish, they could not have survived; happily for them, these two resources were abundant.

The beginning of herding and agriculture

Did the people of the Reindeer Age herd animals? Some prehistorians believe that the horse was already domesticated, but this has not been proven. The peoples who, in the recent past, had an economic system comparable to that of the Reindeer Age knew neither herding nor agriculture.

It's possible to imagine, at the most, that at certain times of the year human groups were linked to herds of wild reindeer, which they followed in their migrations and from which they derived food. This one-way association might have been an intermediate step between hunting and herding proper: To follow the movements of a herd from which one seeks food is already a step toward domestication.

For agriculture, the answer is even clearer. The organization of a farming society requires an economic structure impossible during the Reindeer Age, and also, as we just saw, there were no plants in France that could be cultivated for a constant food supply. The most that we may imagine is a rudimentary caring for food plants that developed naturally, perhaps by getting rid of weeds. Agriculture might have started in certain areas by the weeding of natural vegetation.

The search for minerals

In regions where flint abounds, obtaining raw materials did not pose serious problems. Still, the toolmaker had to dig to the proper depth and choose flint nodules that had not been subject to freezing. If you have ever tried to find flint good enough to chip, you will understand the difficulties this presents. Today, we have cleared land to search in. It must have been much more difficult to find the places to dig for flint when the area was covered by forest or grass. No doubt, the good places were known by tradition; the areas maintained from generation to generation. In certain regions, the flint layers on the surface of the soil are literally covered with flakes and tools from all periods, from the Acheulian to the Bronze Age.

We have seen that the yield in useful cutting edge in a kilo of raw material increased considerably during the Reindeer Age, and for that reason human sites are often found far from the sources of flint. This leads us to think that long treks were undertaken from time to time to look for the large quantities of the raw material necessary for the group; and that real trade probably also existed. Scientists have been studying the microscopic structure of the flints at several sites to determine their geographic origin, but these investigations have not yet given definite results.

Other finds, however, give us information about the objects carried over long distances. The people of the Reindeer

Here, from left to right, is a shell grooved to hang from a thong, a pendant cut out of bone, and two views of a cowrie shell, all found in several levels of the Upper Paleolithic. Marine shells were very much sought after during the Upper Paleolithic, and caves near the shore yield great quantities, pierced with holes to make pendants, necklaces, hair ornaments. It is very strange to see that at Arcy, several hundred kilometers from the sea, we find the same shells, pierced and sawed, that the men of the Reindeer Age later found as fossil shells in the sands around Paris.

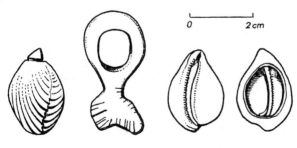

Age collected shells; they pierced them to make hair ornaments or necklaces from them. Some were shells from the seacoast found hundreds of kilometers inland. Others were fossil shells, small ammonites or trilobites, such as the one, pierced as a pendant, that gave its name to one of Arcy-sur-Cure's caves. Many of the Arcy shells certainly came from the sands of the Paris region, about one hundred kilometers away. We can also find pebbles from distant areas collected for their sparkle or their crystals. A magical value was probably attributed to these objects. Their presence in excavations shows that the people of the Reindeer Age sometimes went on long trips.

Cooking

All that we know on the subject of cooking techniques is that many hearths existed. But we don't know of any container, ladle, or spoon. Perhaps there were containers made of bark or skin, spoons made of wood or horn. We just don't know.

Perhaps the people of the Reindeer Age ate their food without cooking it, like some Eskimos who, due to lack of fuel, consume raw, sometimes frozen meat and fish. Perhaps they did as some Native Americans who, without a knowledge of pottery, put heated stones in their bark pots and made excellent broth. Perhaps, like the Australian aborigines, they practiced broiling and baking under the ashes. It's possible that they combined the three systems.

Clothing

To judge from the sewing tools we have found, people of the Reindeer Age probably made clothing out of skins. But the art of the period doesn't give a clear answer.

We have found large numbers of statuettes and bas-reliefs, engravings representing men or women. The women wear no clothing. We cannot conclude from this that they necessarily walked about in this way. Future scientists who, ten thousand years from now, discover one of our contemporary art museums, might make the same sort of mistake about women's fashions in the twentieth century.

As to the masculine figures, the same thing is true: The lines of the face are drawn forward in a type of snout. Several masculine figures wear horns or antlers. Are they shamans, or hunters disguised as animals to deceive the game? Are they supernatural beings, mythological heroes? One found in the Trois-Frères Cave in Ariège, southern France, is an assemblage of parts of animal bodies: antler and ears of a reindeer, face of a snow owl, human hands (?), body of a horse, human legs and feet, horse's tail, human phallus (?). It is not very important whether the figure is that of a god with the body of a man, of reindeer and horse combined, or of a man disguised as a god with the attributes of three animals.

Dwellings

Because the best sites were discovered in caves, we tend to think, sometimes wrongly, that the men of prehistory usually chose this kind of place to live. In reality, dwellings in the open air probably would have been more numerous than those in caves. In the regions where caves are found, they were a good choice as long as they had good exposure and they offered protection against the elements and wild animals. We've begun to realize over the past four years that the cave or rock shelter could provide a second roof for open-air-type dwellings erected under the overhang of the

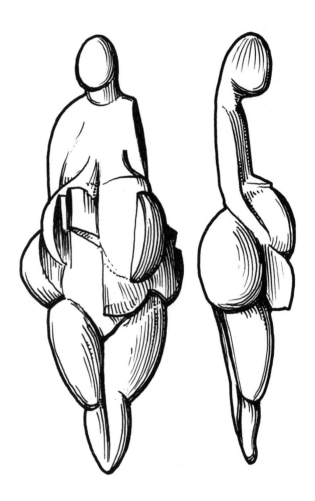

This statuette of mammoth ivory is the most extraordinary of the Paleolithic. It is extremely stylized, and its shape is probably not any more typical of Paleolithic women than certain modern sculptures are typical of the average modern women.

cave. Remains of these huts may be better preserved than those in the open and furnish more information about how advanced in technique the builders were. Thus, at Arcy-sur-Cure, protected by the overhang of the Cave of the Reindeer, the Chatelperronians built and rebuilt circular huts three meters in diameter, with a floor of flat stones, over the course of at least 5,000 years. Part of the framework of these huts might have consisted of mammoth tusks set in holes, and the roof might have been made of skins or bark, flat stones or lumps of soil. These dwellings are different from those of prehistoric Russia and the Ukraine—true pit houses whose construction required skeletal parts of almost 150 mammoths!

We still know very little of the different types of construction that follow one another during the 30,000 years of the Upper Paleolithic. They may have been quite varied, but it is only recently that systematic research has been carried out on the remains of huts, tents, or shacks and that new excavation methods allow us to gain fresh insights from sites formerly considered insignificant. We now know that, under favorable conditions, dwelling sites may be extraordinarily well preserved. This happened at a site in Pincevent in northern France where I studied the remains of a group of reindeer hunters who returned to it regularly. The traces of encampment are on different levels, each of which corresponds to a dwelling unit. The similarity of structures from one level to another allows us to create a typical model, that of a conical tent, slightly oval, with a hearth near the entrance. Ochre forms a carpet around the hearth. Behind this hearth, in a semicircle, is an area of activity where the red soil is strewn with new or used tools; the remaining space

A group of mammoth tusks as it appeared in an excavation. We see an enormous male tusk, a piece of another large tusk, and a female tusk, smaller and straighter. Great quantities of these remains were discovered in the Chatelperronian layers of Arcy, and probably served to construct dwellings. (Photograph A. Leroi-Gourhan)

probably was a sleeping area. Food and domestic refuse accumulated outside the tent. The upkeep of the dwelling was well illustrated in the refuse heaps in which residues of flint manufacture, bones of game animals (99 percent reindeer), and the split stones caused by hearth fire were mixed.

Traces of the base of a circular hut of the Chatelperronian period (40,000 years before our era). The flat stones surround a central space of compacted red-colored earth. Part of the building materials were used by later generations to construct their own similar dwellings. (Photograph M. Sauter)

Reconstruction of a tent of the Late Magdalenian culture (approximately 10,000 to 12,000 years before our era). Poles reconstruct the framework of a tent, only traces of which remain on the floor. At the entrance we see the hearth full of stones, which probably served for cooking by a method in which heated stones are immersed in liquid to make it boil. Behind the hearth, we find an almost empty surface, which must have been shielded at the time by the tent. The ashes, the waste of flint working, and the bones of food animals have been thrown out. Everything that was made of wood or skin has disappeared, leaving, in some cases, empty spots on the floor. The visible containers in this drawing, as well as the poles and the skins for bedding in the back of the tent, are reconstructed.

It's not rare to find a dwelling built against a cliff or rock shelter, protected by the rocky overhang. These are often more comfortable than caves. Finally (but least importantly), men lived in caves themselves. The soil was generally flattened, and to avoid humidity, a layer of stones covered the floor, sometimes amounting to a sort of pavement. Small bits of debris, such as broken or worn tools, broken pendants, scraps of meals lost in the sweepings, piled up on this surface. The soil brought in on the feet of the inhabitants progressively covered these traces to form thin layers that now can be classified in chronological order.

Life was concentrated at the entrance of the cave; the inhabited part rarely extended deeper than thirty meters from the entrance. Here is where the hearths were constructed. Plant fuel must have been difficult to come by, because we find little in the way of plant ashes but large quantities of charred reindeer bones. Once rid of their flesh, broken and emptied of their marrow, these bones fed the fire. The fuel was used carefully: We found ashes sometimes spread out over several square meters, but the hearth itself is most often no larger than a table napkin. It was sometimes dug into the soil, slightly rimmed by stones. Like any open hearth, it was used for cooking, lighting, and heating all at the same time. Traces of an ingenious device for heating were found in several places: The hearth was covered with a pile of pebbles when the embers were still very hot. These stones retained the heat and slowly released it over time. This system is similar to wood-burning stoves in the cold regions of Europe and the "sauna" of the Finns, where you take steam baths by pouring water on heated stones.

The hearth was not alone in providing light. We have numerous Magdalenian lamps, very similar to those of some Eskimos. These lamps were stones, hollowed out to various depths, filled with fat, in which a wick burned. The cave inhabitants also used torches, in particular torches of the juniper tree, because these torches left traces when they were rubbed against a wall to trim them or snuff them out. These lighting devices were used during excursions deep inside the caves, to the recesses where the artists painted their frescoes.

Art and religion

If the men of the Reindeer Age had a system of religious beliefs, we would be hard put to describe it. It would be like describing Christianity only from studying crosses and church statues.

Our evidence in caves consists of objects that go beyond simple practical utility, but it's not possible to sort out mythology from art. For instance:

- red ochre is found in almost all burials, even though it is in no way necessary in burying a corpse
- engravings on harpoons, though a nondecorated harpoon can kill salmon just as well
- pierced shells and teeth, or those with a groove for hanging on a thread or a thong, though one can live comfortably without a shell necklace
- the female statuettes, and the paintings and engravings found in the depths of caves, which in no way improve living conditions or provide food.

When we have inventoried all of this, we become aware that the preoccupations of men of the Reindeer Age go clearly beyond the strictly material. But to distinguish which belong to art, to religion, or to magic raises difficult philosophical problems. We must simply be satisfied with describing the objects.

Over the past few years, important progress has been made in studies of art and religion, and the most striking

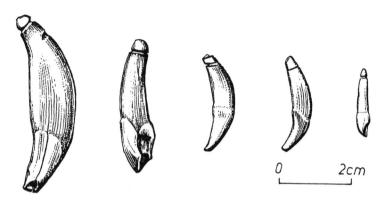

These teeth with grooves for hanging belonged, in order, to the wolf, bison, arctic fox (2), and reindeer. It is difficult to know if they were decorative, symbolic, or both.

aspect of the thinking of Paleolithic hunters is the developments linked to these areas: The famous paintings of the Lascaux Cave are often compared to the masterpieces of Classical art; the horses of the Angles-sur-Anglin bas-reliefs to those of the Greek Parthenon; the ornamented caves to temples. Remember, the most recent of these works had already been created 10,000 years ago, that is, at a distance in time four times that which separates us from the beginning of Greek art.

It is certain that the men of the Upper Paleolithic had a highly developed system of beliefs, expressed in symbolic images related to the world of hunting. It was long believed that the animals represented prey, whose portrait was "killed" and so, by magic, the animal itself. The detailed study of some one hundred ornamented caves in France and Spain revealed that, although the caves don't follow the rules of modern composition and perspective, the positions of the images could not be explained solely by chance.

The shape of the cave itself often shows that the placement of figures was important. The choice of the best panel for a "monumental" composition, such as the large ceilings of Altamira in Spain, Rouffignac in France, Ekaïn in Spain, which are then covered with animal figures in careful relationship to one another, cannot be explained by chance. The kind and number of animals represented seems to follow rules.

The numerical sequence. The number of horses or ibexes compared to the total number of animals represented seems to demonstrate such principles. The most pictured species are the horse (A) (30 percent) and the great bovines, bison or aurochs (B) (30 percent), which together seem to constitute the main part of the composition; in third place (C), the deer and doe (11 percent), then the mammoth (9 percent), the ibex (8 percent), and the reindeer (3.5 percent).

The painted ceiling of the Altamira Cave contains about twenty bisons, facing for the most part toward the left. Around the edge of the herd (colored black for emphasis) are, from left to right, two does, another within a horse, a large head of a horse, and a boar.

The fourth group (D) concerns dangerous animals, clearly in the minority: bear, felines, rhinoceros (approximately 1 percent for each). The spatial organization of the representation in the cave corresponds to an A-B C-D scheme. The grouping consists of a central theme (AB) (horse-bison), which may, as in Altimira, Spain, include more than twenty bisons bordered by two horses accompanied by two does (C). One very large doe (E) on the edge is a solitary presence. At the other end of the ceiling a boar occupies a D position, that is, a dangerous animal.

At Ekaïn (Guipuzcoa, Spain), the situation is reversed. On the large ceiling of the cave, the central area is occupied by horses (A), one of which faces to the right. Three bisons (B), one of which faces left, occupy a surface above them, turning away from the horses. On the right margin there is a large doe (C); above, one finds an ibex (C); a fish (a rare theme) occupies a position on the left edge. A ceiling or

In the cave at Ekaïn (Spain) the number of horses to bisons are in reverse proportions to those at Altamira.

large wall surface makes it possible to display the animals in relative positions. We can see, as in the case of Les Trois-Frères or in Lascaux, the hierarchy of the large animals A and B, bordered by the animals C and D (or only C). When the usable surface is long and narrow, the figures follow one another and the elements C and D may be out of the central panel and in a peripheral position. The deer and ibex are relegated to a smaller gallery. There are many examples where a pair of male ibexes (C) frames a bovine (Niaux) or deer (Las Monedas, Santander). There are still many problems to be resolved to understand the manner in which the art was organized, but we are beginning to know what questions must be asked.

The list of the animals represented on walls is shorter than for those depicted on bone artifacts. On walls horse-bison plus ibex is the most widely distributed assemblage. Horse and bison (or auroch) make up the basic formula, but examples of just these two species are rare. In one case, the two figures are located face to face on two walls.

The animal C is not always the same; and it may be doubled or tripled. One cave has the formula A (horse), B (auroch), C (ibex), with the deer present in all the groupings and the mammoth present only in the first group of engravings.

The most dangerous animals—bear, large felines, and rhinoceros—have positions at the edge of the engraved panels (Les Trois-Frères), in the grouping farthest away from the entrance (Lascaux), or simply at the end of the grouping (Labastide).

The representations in decorated caves are not hunting tallys, but they show the relationship among the symbols,

The "mammoth with raised trunk" is one of the eighteen engravings in the Cave of the Horse, at Arcy. These engravings were executed as a group, in two halls, at the back of an almost inaccessible passageway, one hundred meters from the entrance. Most of them take their form from the curves of the wall, like this mammoth head, where the eye and the hair were worked with a burin to emphasize a natural hollow in the wall.

which correspond to a structured mythology. This idea is reinforced by the study of signs.

Signs. Animal figures are not alone on the walls. There are also geometric signs of varied shapes. These signs have not attracted much attention from prehistorians, who have been satisfied with vague comparisons with traps, huts, boomerangs, wounds; but these interpretations are without foundation other than a general coincidence of shape, at best, in a few cases.

The signs are of three kinds: narrow signs (stick, hook, barbed line . . .), full signs (triangles, ovals, rectangles), punctuated signs (dots in a line, in a figure . . .). The narrow signs and the full signs seem to be geometric abstractions of sexual organs, which at first were realistic representations that evolved through time to become symbolic. The full signs have strong regional variants, and we wonder whether the symbols themselves did not come to stand for different populations. We could thus understand very well why the cave, which all people considered a symbol of maternity, would carry hidden in it the emblems of the group.

The narrow signs accompany the full signs in a very inconspicuous manner; they are often related to the shape of the wall itself, such as an oval cavity whose interior is painted with red ochre, a barbed sign in a narrow area.

The relations between signs and animal figures have not been subject to research. But they may be closely related, as at Lascaux, where the signs are integrated with the animal decor of different parts of the cave.

The lines of punctuation generally function as borders. They are found in series of anywhere from a few dots to several dozens, at the beginning and end of groupings. We

Coupled signs. No. 1 shows some of the original female symbolism. No. 2 is reduced to a four-sided figure (full sign), accompanied by two dashes (narrow sign). No. 3 is made up of rectangles accompanied by punctuated lines.

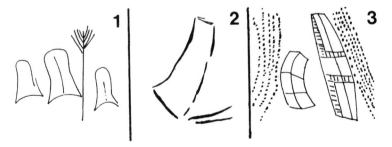

also see them at Pech-Merle on the contours and in the interiors of dappled horses; and at two caves in the Ariège they are drawn by a thumb on clay in wavy outlines.

These few pages on signs show the complexity of the problem of Paleolithic art. We see that the questions asked are far from being answered. It is probable that Paleolithic man possessed a developed spiritual life. What remains today is only the skeleton of the myth.

Ochre

Iron oxide ochre is relatively common, particularly in the limestone regions where caves are found. The last of the Mousterians began to use it, and from the beginning of the Perigordian or Aurignacian it is common. Its color varies from yellow to red to brown, depending on the mineral content and on whether it is used raw or burned. Ochre is one of the basic colors used by the cave painters. Doubtless it also had other uses we poorly understand.

We often find fragments of ochre cut into points, like pencils, or pieces ground into facets, or flat pebbles upon which the coloring material was crushed. This leads us to suppose that many other things were colored with red besides the cave paintings. Perhaps men painted their faces, like the Australians or Native Americans; perhaps they painted their weapons, like the Eskimos of Alaska; perhaps they drew on hides or bark, like many recent peoples.

In a certain number of burials of the Reindeer Age, we find the skeleton immersed in a layer of ochre and colored red. Was ochre the symbol of blood and life, a means of protecting oneself against a dead person, an offering given to him to protect the living against his vengeance? In any case, here is evidently a rite with religious significance.

Finally, we find ochre strewn on the floors of dwellings. At certain sites, we are struck by the intensity of this red coloration. At Arcy-sur-Cure the layer that corresponds to the middle Aurignacian is truly extraordinary: A layer ten to twenty centimeters deep of almost pure red-purple ochre rests on the very clear paving stones of the inhabited space. This layer is mixed with the tiny debris of everyday life. The ochre was brought from about one kilometer away, on the other side of the river, in loads of several hundred kilos. Was it all spread at one time to make a kind of carpet for the dwelling, or was it used a few kilos at a time to freshen up the beautiful red ochre rug? What was the meaning of this flood of color? It is possible that red, symbol of blood, was a magical symbol and a sign of wealth for these ancient hunters. Ochre may also have been used in the preparation of skins.

Burials

Several dozen burials of the Reindeer Age have been discovered in Europe. The dead body is sometimes contracted, sometimes extended; stones sometimes protect its head and there is always a pit. Most often the body was buried with ornaments: a cup of shell ornaments on the head, necklaces, and a few bone or flint objects.

To leave the dead body with the personal objects of the living person supposes that someone is afraid of being contaminated by death, or fears vengeance from the dead, or that one gives him equipment for another world. Magical contamination through objects does not necessarily imply an afterlife, though a religious connotation is suggested. The other two hypotheses imply belief in an afterlife. The protection given to the head seems also to indicate that the men of this age did not consider the dead to be devoid of all human faculties.

Decorated objects

We find javelins, harpoons, spear throwers, pierced *bâtons,* and awls by the hundreds engraved and sculpted with figures, most often representing animals. It's possible that ideas of magic inspired these works: A spear decorated with reindeer could reach this animal more easily than an undecorated one. But it is also likely that the artist worked for his pleasure, that art went beyond religious life into everyday life, without a clear separation.

Decorated portable artifacts are divided into two large categories. The first category is further subdivided into durable objects and fragile objects. The subcategory of fragile objects is made up of short-lived artifacts, spear points in particular, which often break up in the body of the animal or against a stone; these often bear very simple geometric decorations. On the other hand, the more durable objects, the pierced *bâtons,* the spear throwers, the half-cylindrical wands—elongated objects with convex, decorated backs and flat undersurfaces grooved to facilitate adhesion (to what is still unknown)—bear a decoration that is often in bas-relief and done with care.

The division of portable objects into these two categories, based on use, reflects the creation by Paleolithic people of two modes of expression, one where the animal forms are elaborated and detailed, the other where the abbreviation is pushed to the maximum, leading to forms that are similar to the pictographic symbols of ancient Chinese writing or the cuneiform writing of the Near East. But Paleolithic men did not possess true writing, since there is no evidence of a succession of pictographs ordered in a structured sequence.

The second major category consists of plaques made of stone or bone, which were engraved or painted with designs similar to those on the ceilings and walls of caves. We do not yet know their meaning.

Sanctuary caves

Approximately 150 "decorated caves" have been discovered so far. All (except one, Kapova Cave, at the foot of the Ural mountains) are located in France, in Spain, and less commonly in Italy. The caves are varied in form and dimension.

People were attracted to rock shelters exposed to daylight as well as to shallow caves. We shall never know how many masterpieces were destroyed in these cases by natural causes. The caves that were a little deeper insured some security for the works on their walls. In even deeper caves, engravings and paintings begin only at the last point where natural light is still visible. This fact is not necessarily linked to philosophical thinking, but is probably due to caution, so the painter could escape if his torch or lamp went out. During the Aurignacian and Upper Perigordian (30,000 to 20,000 years ago), these walls of caves just a little deeper may have saved the most ancient works. In most cases, the artwork in caves is relatively accessible, but some show that the Magdalenians did not worry about danger if there was a spectacular location. Some caves were narrow crawl spaces in their original state. Sometimes the floor has been lowered in present times to accommodate tourists. The passageway-caves of moderate length are not too dangerous in case of loss of light; but this is not so in those caves that are made up of mazes, especially in large caves with many branches.

The introduction of the cave into religious life is a characteristic of Paleolithic men. As the art style evolved, decoration reached farther into the great depths of the caves during the Middle Magdalenian and came back to the entrance during the Upper Magdalenian. In caves that present real difficulties, traces of visitors or even occasional passage are rare. From the Magdalenian to the seventeenth century, ten thousand years of silence reign over them.

10

The End
of Prehistoric Times

The last glaciation has reached its end. About 8,000 years before our era, the last reindeer have definitely taken the road to the north. The temperate Atlantic climate, familiar to us, follows the cold. The steppe and the taiga, full of horses and reindeer, are replaced by hazel trees and beautiful forests of oak and beech, traveled only by small groups of red deer, roe deer, and boar. From then on, game plays only a secondary role in nutrition, only up to 30 percent of the meat diet for certain groups.

The whole long epoch studied in this book—from the obscure beginnings of humanity to the end of the Reindeer Age—is included by prehistorians under the name Paleolithic, that is "Old Stone Age." Then the Neolithic, or "New Stone Age," opens, a time also of the first metalworking. Between the two is a "middle age," the Mesolithic.

The Mesolithic in France left fewer traces than the Mousterian in the Reindeer Age. Humanity fell to a very much lower economic and cultural level. During the Reindeer Age, western Europe was one of the great zones of civilization, as evidenced by the cave-sanctuaries of France and Spain. During the Mesolithic, the important events take place elsewhere: in the north toward the Baltic, where climatic conditions are the same as they had been earlier in France, and especially more to the south, in the eastern Mediterranean, where the civilizations of the historic times are already beginning. We are very near the time when, in these regions, agriculture and herding, metalworking and writing appear one after another. In France during this time small groups of men are settled on the edge of rivers or on beaches, still living from fishing and food gathering. A few, in the Pyrenees and in Provence, gather snails and seafood in significant amounts.

About 3,000 years before our era, Neolithic culture, based on agriculture and herding, reaches western Europe. Between 2,500 and 2,000 years before our era, the first copper objects appear in France, soon followed by bronze. But here the prehistorian begins to give up the floor to the historian, for in this book we only wanted to sketch the developments of the Paleolithic.

The Paleolithic represents a whole stage of humanity. From the archanthropians manufacturing choppers to *Homo sapiens sapiens* covering the walls of the Lascaux Cave with decoration, we follow the hunting culture across changes of men and climates. This world lasted at least one hundred times longer than ours has, and now it seems to us that it existed on another planet: It is as dead as its monsters, the mammoths and woolly rhinoceroses. Afterward, all of culture will be constructed upon different bases: Grain will demand a granary, the granary will require walls for defense and soldiers to protect the walls, a scribe to count the wheat sacks, impose taxes, and write history. If *Homo sapiens* had appeared at the same time as grain, we might think that these two worlds belonged to different kinds of humanity, that they had nothing to do one with the other. But we now know that, before playing the first act of contemporary times, *Homo sapiens,* our fellow man, had first played the last act of the preceding scene, that is of Paleolithic times.

Without the science of prehistory, the most marvelous and also the most mysterious aspect of our destiny would escape us. Present historic times represent only a few minutes in the long journey of mankind; if we knew them only, we would ignore the stubborn struggle that man pursued in the search for his achievements.

If the excavators of caves had not been able to make Neanderthals, like our Augustine, tell their tale, we would have false ideas about the childhood of humanity. Our Augustine did not understand much about philosophy or trade, but she knew the labors of her time. She may have had the brain of a three-year-old in a large body that was neither slim nor supple, but doesn't the three-year-old child possess, in an obscure way, the qualities that will be those of the adult?

To study prehistory because we're curious about the odds and ends of broken pebbles and bones would be a vain occupation. Birds that sing and streams that flow are really more attractive. But to take advantage of what we know about past times so as better to understand what man is, is surely to honor the billions of beings who died after transmitting to their descendants the secret of making a biface, until the day when their successors decided, a bit too quickly, that they had become wise men.

Index